D0390986

PARENTING
THE NEW TEEN
IN THE AGE
OF ANXIETY

Purchased from
Multnomah County Library
Title Wave Used Bookstore
216 NE Knott St. Portland, OR
503-988-5021

PARENTING THE NEW TEEN IN THE AGE OF ANXIETY

A Complete Guide to Your Child's
Stressed, Depressed, Expanded,
Amazing Adolescence

DR. JOHN DUFFY

Mango Publishing
CORAL GABLES

Copyright © 2019 by Dr. John Duffy.
Published by Mango Publishing Group, a division of Mango Media Inc.

Cover Design: Roberto Núñez
Layout & Design: Roberto Núñez

Mango is an active supporter of authors' rights to free speech and artistic expression in their books. The purpose of copyright is to encourage authors to produce exceptional works that enrich our culture and our open society.

Uploading or distributing photos, scans or any content from this book without prior permission is theft of the author's intellectual property. Please honor the author's work as you would your own. Thank you in advance for respecting our author's rights.

For permission requests, please contact the publisher at:
Mango Publishing Group
2850 S Douglas Road, 2nd Floor
Coral Gables, FL 33134 USA
info@mango.bz

For special orders, quantity sales, course adoptions and corporate sales, please email the publisher at sales@mango.bz. For trade and wholesale sales, please contact Ingram Publisher Services at customer.service@ingramcontent.com or +1.800.509.4887.

Parenting the New Teen in the Age of Anxiety: Complete Guide to Your Child's Stressed, Depressed, Expanded, Amazing Adolescence

Library of Congress Cataloging-in-Publication number: 2019944131
ISBN: (print) 978-1-64250-049-3, (ebook) 978-1-64250-050-9
BISAC category code PSYCHOLOGY / Developmental / Adolescent

Printed in the United States of America

Note: When discussing parenting issues herein that are not gender-specific, I have chosen to use the female pronoun. Unless otherwise specified, stories and advice are not intended to apply to any one gender.

For Julie

Table of Contents

FOREWORD

We are all aware of how challenging it is today to raise our kids. The pressure parents are confronted with is unprecedented. But it pales in comparison to the profound emotional impact of recent technological, social, cultural, and academic stressors on our children, and all of the overwhelming anxiety and depression they are suffering at shockingly early ages. John's new book is a user-friendly guide through the morass, and it will help you maintain a strong, positive, and joyful connection with your child.

Already at only seven-years-old, our son Duke's world is unrecognizable to us. He is bombarded with so much more data and stimulation than we were, and therefore has so much more on his emotional and intellectual plate. We are so excited to have this timely and powerful resource to help us now, and provide us strategies for what lies ahead.

We've known John on a personal and professional level for many years. He is our go-to for parenting and relationship questions. His advice is always honest, constructive, solid, and enlightening.

John is the real deal. He works with parents and kids in his practice every day. He knows what kids are dealing with, what their struggles are, where their strengths lie, what they know, and what they need.

Every parent needs to read this book. John gives parents a deep, clear understanding of our children's world and gives them tools to help navigate and thrive through it all.

GIULIANA AND BILL RANCIC
E! News anchor and entrepreneur, respectively

PREFACE

I love writing. I really do. And several years ago, I experienced the good fortune of knocking a large, significant item off my personal bucket list: I published a book. Not only that, I felt as if I published an important book, one that mattered, one that would, if taken seriously, drive a significant positive change in the lives of families, specifically those of teenagers and their parents.

I told stories. I dispelled myths. I drew from many years of direct clinical work, and came up with a truly user-friendly framework for parents of teenagers, one that I knew turned some of the more traditional models and belief systems about teens on their heads. I was proud of it, and still am. I had my say and, as far as I was concerned, I was done with the matter. I freed myself to move on to write something lighter, perhaps existential and Eastern-derived, more philosophical than psychological, something a little more Nietzsche and a little less niche-y.

(Apologies for that. Couldn't resist.)

In any event, this shift in focus was not meant to be. Here am I to address that parent-teen relationship once again, in full recognition that, in the fleeting few years between publication of *The Available Parent* and the present, the world of our teens and of their parents has changed so dramatically, so thoroughly, that the subject requires revisiting.

I am finding that parenting today is a more urgent matter than it was even those few short years ago. The stakes are higher, the dangers greater, the threats to self-worth and self-esteem wildly more pervasive.

And what looks like misbehavior, checking out, dropping out, refusing to go, are most likely overcorrections, adaptive mechanisms to relieve the stress of the perfectionistic, hyper-driven AP student, crushing it while secretly cutting herself for relief, or sneaking a Juul or weed break after her parents are fast asleep. These days, no child escapes childhood unscathed. Our generation by and large created this dynamic. It is ours to fix. We owe it to our kids.

For the stress is truly absurd and immeasurable, and the shift toward a manageable teenage life is the new mandate, imperative for all parents of teens or soon-to-be-teens.

So, help a guy out. I'm a writer. I've got ideas, maybe a novel or a play in me. Help me make this the last book I write on parenting.

Please.

NOTE TO PARENTS

I have enormous admiration for this generation of teenagers. They are kind and they are thoughtful, and they are worldly. They have a sense of justice that I don't remember having a concept of when I was their age. They are exposed to the harshest elements of the world much too soon. If I could reverse some of that for their growing minds, I would. But the upside is that we are unwittingly raising wonderful people who have this thoughtful, compassionate worldview that we may have lacked.

I personally didn't have much of a point of view at age eight, eleven, even seventeen. Today, I don't know many kids who don't have a distinct point of view. Our job is to help them make sense of and integrate all they take in. And to do that, we must know and truly understand their world so we can collaborate with them.

Our kids are in an undue degree of psychic pain and they need an open dialogue. If we can get them talking, we can help ease their anxious minds.

For parents, the idea is understanding. So that when your kid is overwhelmed (and your kid is going to feel overwhelmed), when your kid is exposed to too much (and your kid will be exposed to too much), she will know: I have Mom and/or Dad, and they are my constants, they are solid. I can go to them and they are going to hear me out, without judgment. I *know* that. I know that I can talk to them and they are going to be there for me unequivocally. And in this nutty world with all of these stimuli, kids need *some* compass. They need you to be that compass.

It's natural for us as parents, when anxieties rise, to try to clamp down and control our child, or maybe look the other way because we are afraid to deal with their struggles. We sometimes want to spare ourselves and our children the difficult conversations because we think it's too early, or that bringing up the topic will be "planting a seed," whether it's about drinking, or sex, or drugs, depression, anxiety, or suicide—any of these tough topics. But we do not have that option anymore. We have to be open and curious and engaged and in the trenches with them. We need to be actively learning about their world so that when they need us, we *get* it.

Now, I know you are busy, and that parenting is not your sole role in life, nor the sole source of stress. I am fully aware that you face your own set of challenges that involve your life, your relationships, your work and finances, and dreams, and so on. I get that.

I prelude this book with these thoughts because you are about to read, in great detail, about a whole new landscape for teenagers, and for children around the teen years.

And it all starts earlier, and runs longer, than you think.

Some of this stuff will feel quite difficult to read. Some of it is heavy. We are going to talk, in depth, about depression and anxiety, suicidality and loneliness, and sex and drugs. Some of the mandates I'm asking you to fulfill are difficult and may run against the grain of your parenting instincts.

I wrote this book for two reasons.

First, I think that, in order to be an effective, available parent today—in order to guide your child through the "new adolescence"—you need to be more fully informed, more "woke," than any other generation of parents preceding you. Because there is no blueprint, I am attempting to provide one here.

And you will find my advice to be strikingly consistent:

- Talk to your children in an open and ongoing discussion, free of lectures.

- Pump up the balance in the Emotional Bank Account you maintain with your child, so that your words carry weight with them.

- Ask open-ended questions about issues they may well be struggling with that you are either unaware of, or do not fully understand.

- Inform yourself, frequently.

- Maintain your precious connection with your child, always.

This basic methodology will, believe it or not, consume less of your time, not more. And it will spare you, your child, and your entire family untold heartache for countless years—seriously. You will feel armed to serve as the ally, guide, and consultant your child needs to navigate the newly uncharted waters of a stressful, anxiety-provoking, and prolonged adolescent journey.

The other reason is to provide you with hope.

If you follow the guidelines I offer, I am confident that things will work out. That's not to suggest you and your child will not encounter bumps and bruises along the path. These are not only inevitable, they are important. We will see that they provide the opportunities for the development of the competence and resilience your child needs to manage their world, to thrive.

So please, as you read on, do not be discouraged. There is a lot here. But if you follow the protocol, you can enjoy their adolescence together, and each challenge can bring you closer together, instead of rending you apart.

And your connection is so very important. The most painful moments in my office arise not when a family is in the midst of crisis. The most painful moments are those in which I bear witness to a parent losing their child in real time, right before my eyes, needlessly.

There is a lot of work to do. But there is good news here, too. If you read carefully and follow the guidelines offered, you are fostering the well-being of a unique and brilliant child—your child. As you will find, even if it is not yet wholly apparent to you, your child possesses a degree of depth, intelligence, and empathy that will move our world in the right direction.

Change is coming rapidly toward our children. I am grateful that you have picked up this book. Your child will be far better off for it, as will you. As will we all.

So, thank you.

Part One

PAINTING THE PICTURE

Jason's Story: What Are We Missing?

Jason is sixteen years old. He is bright and personable. He has a job he does well and shows respect for the paycheck he draws. He is an Honor Roll student, popular and handsome. He also manages the awkward setup of a therapy room with unusual grace. He can pick up the trickiest guitar leads by ear, eliciting no small degree of jealousy from his rusty therapist. By all accounts, life is good for Jason. He frequently cites that he has grown up privileged: nice house, plenty of money, generally sweet and loving parents. A seemingly uneventful coming-of-age story.

Jason has also, however, done two separate stints in inpatient therapy, one for suicidal ideation with clear intent to harm himself, the other for marked drug abuse. The drugs he ingested ranged from alcohol to marijuana, Benadryl in excess, Klonopin, Oxycodone, and a host of other prescription drugs, along with the occasional use of "club drugs" including Ecstasy and LSD. At one point, an ER doctor reported to Jason's parents that he had been hours, if not minutes, from death when his ambulance arrived.

Now, you might be wondering how Jason, with this great life and this loving family, could possibly have ended up in these terrifying, life-threatening situations.

It's a reasonable question.

Parents today are very involved—far, far more involved in the lives of their children than our parents were even a generation ago. Today, there are parent conferences, conventions, and

Parent Universities. There are books and online groups and clubs and apps, all directing us toward improved parenting. I have had the good fortune to speak at many of these events, and to participate on many of these platforms. And lately, with permission, I have shared Jason's story. The parental responses often surprise me:

"Clearly, his parents aren't on it. Otherwise, they would know he isn't okay."

"This is on the parents. They must be missing the mark and selling you a bill of goods about being good parents."

"This kid needs to take responsibility for his actions."

"He needs a swift kick in the ass."

But I can tell you with total assurance that these comments are missing the larger picture. For this is not just Jason's story. This is, in many ways, the story of countless teenage boys and girls, both younger and older than you might think possible, across the country, across demographics, across socioeconomic strata.

This could be your child.

And the conventional solutions miss the mark as well, and are not really solutions at all.

Let me tell you more about Jason. He was a stellar athlete in grammar school, but quit sports around sixth grade. He earned straight A's until roughly that same time. He hung out with friends, perfected moves on his skateboard, and tells idyllic stories of vacations with his family. He was the Academic All-American, the kid you *want*.

By junior high, as his parents describe it, the wheels started
to wobble. He was looking down at his phone, engulfed in
Snapchat and Instagram, overinvested in numbers of likes
and views. He became deeply ensconced in video games,
about which they knew nothing other than that they seemed
unreasonably violent, and he seemed flat-out addicted to
playing them. The rest of the time, he skulked up to his room
and shut the door, the remainder of his day and evening
shrouded in mystery.

Now, as far as they were concerned, Jason's parents weren't
negligent. They were worried about him, so they tracked his
phone whenever he was out, keeping watch over the moving
blip on the map like military drone pilots, ready to strike and
call the mission at any moment that looked dicey. They signed
on daily to the school's grade portal, collecting intel on not only
cumulative grades, but each class skipped, each assignment
missed, each quiz failed. Through a YouTube tutorial, they
reverse-engineered passcodes for his phone and social media,
allowing them real-time access to his texts, social media posts,
and responses. They maintained a store of breathalyzers and
drug tests in the medicine cabinet.

They amassed all the data that could possibly be available
to a parent.

Alas, all they learned was that he was disengaged from school,
disappearing into some "drug culture," and slipping deeper into
connections with his new "low-life, going nowhere" friends.
And he was drifting further and further away from them.
They felt as if, no matter what wisdom they offered, how often
they addressed him in a positive tone, or whatever lightness

they tried to bring to their relationships with him, he was drifting away.

And as far as they were concerned, they were doing it right. They had read my first book diligently. They had attended parenting conferences. Jason's sister had turned out fine, so they were doing something right. They showed enormous faith in him on a regular basis, telling him they knew he could do better, in school, in choosing friends. This was keeping the bar high, right? This was proof that they had faith in him.

But if this method is supposed to work, then where is he, right? Where is our sweet, perfect guy?

Herein lies the quandary for the modern parent. We are scared. We are lost. We are feeling around in the dark, tracking the information we can, hoping to find our child, intact and safe.

Like Jason, today's teenagers are, for the most part, a mystery to us parents. Let's start by solving the mystery, bit by bit, as best we can. Then we can talk about what agency we have as parents to make things better.

And trust me. No matter what issues you might be struggling with, as a parent, as a family, things *can* get better.

You Were Never a Teenager

I worked with a father and son late one evening recently. Dad was earnestly, admirably trying to connect with his struggling son, letting him know he understood what he was going through, and was familiar with his experience. After all, he was sixteen once, and it wasn't *all* that long ago.

But in his son's mind, he never was.

The emotional weight of being a teenager in today's world bears only a faint resemblance to our experiences as teenagers a generation ago. I find that this is a critical concept that is very difficult for parents to understand and accept. Now, when I talk to groups of parents, I receive a lot of pushback on this concept.

"Of course, I was a full-fledged teenager. I felt that emotional weight. I felt that insecurity, in my body, in my personality, in my very being."

And yes, to an extent, we can relate. But the truth is, you were never *this* teenager.

Our teenage concerns, free of the weight of social media "likes," the pace of online chaos, the overarching academic pressures, and the wildly unreasonable body-image demands, are artifacts of an era gone by. All of these factors play into the self-esteem and the daily measurement of self-worth of the typical teenager, tween-aged child, or young adult today.

So, the bad news is that you've got a lot to learn. The good news is that you have teachers, likely right down the hall from you right now. Addressed openly and without an agenda, your children will likely be happy to introduce you to the complications of their daily lives.

And trust me, the stakes are high. You need that introduction into their ever-changing world. And you'll need follow-up as well. Otherwise, you are parenting from a handbook with wildly outdated information. Not only might you be unaware of the nuances of the ills of vaping versus Juuling, but the nature of social pressures, future fears, and sometimes hopelessness may elude you as well.

So, ask the questions that may scare you. Listen to the answers, even if they are not what you want to hear. That way, your child will know you are there for her, to walk by her side, through the unpredictable tangle of adolescence.

Your child needs you. Now more than ever.

I encourage you to go to school on this next generation. Sometime in the car, or during breakfast, or before bed, ask them.

Ask them what their friends are up to these days. Ask about kids their age. Be curious; do not interrogate.

"What are other kids doing? Are they smoking, drinking, vaping? Are they having sex? Is anyone super-depressed, self-harming? Is there anyone you're worried about?"

"How do you feel about it all? What are you doing?"

And most importantly, "How are you doing?"

These may seem like very dramatic questions, but I can virtually promise you, your child will be more comfortable than you are talking about this stuff. And it's crucial that you find that comfort zone in yourself, breathe deeply, ask, and talk. It's the only way I know to create that elusive collaboration with your teenager, and she needs that. With you.

Keep asking. Create an easy, open line of communication. Speak your piece and let her speak hers. Let the resounding thought she's left with be, "No matter what, I've got your back. You can come to me."

This is precisely the approach I encouraged for this dad the other night. I know that, if he follows that advice, he can put me out of business in his son's life quickly and forge that connection and collaboration.

The New Teen

First, believe it or not, we have to revisit what we mean when we use the term "teenager." Since the coining of the term, it has always demarcated a stage of physical development, as well as a shift in self-awareness and emotional development. On the emotional side, the primary challenge faced during adolescence is the establishment of an identity separate and apart from Mom, Dad, and other familiar adults. Historically, the actual teenage years, thirteen to nineteen, have framed this developmental period, both physically and emotionally, quite well. Parents and families have supported this progression over the generations, controlling the flow of information our children take in and assessing what's appropriate for them at different ages. The bolder among us have introduced the topics of sexuality, drug use, social difficulties, and other issues at the onset of these years, and dished out information as deemed developmentally appropriate.

The way the culture was constructed and driven, and the way we have parented in the past, supported the onset of adolescence around thirteen years of age, and the completion of that identity formation, more or less, at about nineteen. There were exceptions, of course, but they were fairly obvious, enough so that the adult cavalry—parents, schools, churches, and neighbors—could intervene and redirect a child toward the appropriate developmental markers, should they stray too far off course.

Now, we are going to find that the "teen" designation is no longer entirely valid, certainly not the way it has been used historically. Because of a combination of unlimited access to information, the advent of social media and other technology, rising academic pressures, and other familial and social stressors, the teen years as we think of them have stretched to well before thirteen on the early end, and beyond nineteen on the back end. Some of those "teenage" discussions—those talks about sex, drugs, depression, anxiety, suicide, events in the news—we need to begin with children at often uncomfortably young ages. We lack the control that we used to have over what young kids might be exposed to, so we must be aware and prepared to address issues and take on discussions that would typically be reserved for much older kids.

We are also witnessing a prolonged adolescence on the back end, as our young adults remain stifled by the overwhelming load of information, emotion, and identity confusion they are processing through the teen years. They remain unclear about their place in the world well into their twenties.

The Disappearance of the Tween

When titling my first book, *The Available Parent*, the word tween carried some distinct meaning, so much so that it was part of my subtitle. This was a preadolescent stage, couched between the ages of ten and twelve or so. But you likely notice, with perhaps a note of alarm, how younger children seem to be adopting the behaviors and attitudes we used to see in tweens and even teens. These include, but are certainly not limited to:

- A draw toward social media

- Development of sexual identity

- Body consciousness

- Mention of feeling depressed or anxious

- Talking back

- Testing boundaries behaviorally

In a sense, the tween years have disappeared, and our children are developmentally sprung from childhood into adolescence without the cushion of a couple of years to get accustomed to new thought patterns and behavioral draws.

As suggested above, we would love to allow for more years of childhood innocence before this adolescent-type behavior and thinking kicks in. But we are dealing with a brand-new reality here, a developmental leap with our younger children in which they skip the cushion of the "tween" years. Given these recent changes, I again encourage you to consider to begin to talk with your younger children, considering their personal maturity and developmental level, about the issues you may have thought were reserved for teens or tweens. Begin to gently work your way toward talking, and asking, about the opposite sex, drug use, insecurities, mental health, and so on. The key here is to let your kids know, earlier than you may think necessary, that you are aware, informed, and available to talk, on any subject, at any time.

The New Early Teen

I have described the above phenomenon, the stretching of adolescence and the resulting fallout, to a number of colleagues and friends. And I have been faced with skepticism, the prevailing question being, "How do I know this seismic shift is actually taking place?"

It's an entirely fair question. What I'm suggesting here is not simply that our children are experiencing more, and taking in more stimuli, at earlier and earlier ages. No, it runs far deeper than that. I'm suggesting that developmental patterns that have stood for decades, if not centuries, have shifted in a matter of just a few years. I'm suggesting that our children are developing a sense of self and awareness of others at much earlier ages than ever before. I'm suggesting that the very nature of childhood is shifting at an unprecedented pace, right under our noses, and very few people are fully aware of either the phenomenon or its potent impact on the totality of a child's life today.

I spent an hour with Jack recently, a deep and thoughtful nineteen-year-old lamenting the apparent generational gap between himself and his brother, only four years his junior. "I worry about Ryan and his generation, man. They have a lot more stress than we did at fifteen. They were born in the iPhone era, and the pressure of social media and all that is in their DNA. We were born just before all that. I can remember that time. We would just play outside all the time. Ryan and his friends are never outside, and they seem so sedated: no hobbies, no interests. They just sit around vaping and joy-sticking their lives away [laughs]. I wish they saw the world more like I do. I see the future, and it's *out there* and big and exciting. Ryan and his dudes, I don't think they get that."

He worries more about his younger sister, only nine, and her generation. "I don't think we have any idea how fast those kids are growing up, right now."

In some form or fashion, I have heard Jack's sentiment expressed with alarming regularity over the course of the past several years. Yes, the very nature of childhood is entirely different, quite suddenly. And if brothers only four years apart sense a gap, we have to recognize the degree to which we ourselves have precious little in common with our children. Given this sudden developmental shift, this sudden leap from childhood to adolescence, we have *everything* to learn. We parents today are true pioneers, whether we choose to be or not. We have to parent with more thought and care, as there are pitfalls we can guide our kids safely beyond if we arm ourselves with sufficient information.

Now, I know it is real, the dramatic nature of this shift, because I have a highly unusual job. I work with these children, many hours a day. And I can tell you, unequivocally, the patterns are not vague. The shift is abundantly clear. And the fallout is overwhelming at best, but devastating in the extreme. Let's review some of the grim realities:

- Children report strikingly more stress now than ever before.

- Poor self-esteem, and a higher degree of self-loathing, are reported by children now more than ever before.

- Body image issues are far more prevalent now than ever before, and at shockingly early ages.

- Substance abuse is on the rise, often in the pursuit of self-medication, and the nature and type of substances used are shape-shifting.

- Suicide rates are skyrocketing among young people.

- We have seen a precipitous rise in school shootings, and other mass shootings, by young people.

So, the urgency to recognize and acknowledge this shift lies in the fact that we are losing children in record numbers, either literally or figuratively. Consider all the talent and joy and contribution lost when just one teen takes their own life. In aggregate, I fear we are heading in a direction in which we lose the gifts of countless young people, even as they continue to draw breath. And we are all the worse for the losses, without a doubt.

For I find that the young people who are vulnerable, who struggle to find value in themselves, and feel their feelings so strongly, are the very people we need most right now. They don't recognize their value, but in reality, it knows no bounds. We have to save them, for their sake and for our own.

Self-Consciousness

Think back to your childhood: a component of the ease of that time was less self-awareness, less insecurity, and few comparisons to others. Younger children didn't consider, to the degree teenagers did, whether other kids were smarter, more athletic, better looking, and so on. For a time, the pace of brain development provided a layer of protection from some of these insecurities. For those of you who were the exception, you know how painful it can be to make those comparisons, as we tend to evaluate ourselves negatively in every respect, "one down" from others.

Now, picture an eight-, nine-, or ten-year-old today. He or she is likely very aware of their "imperfections," real or merely perceived: their bodies, their minds, even the socioeconomic status of their family, relative to their peers. And, like the rest of us, they also tend to make "upward" social comparisons, matching themselves up with children they perceive as "better" than them in whatever aspect of self they are evaluating.

And kids today are exposed to the stimuli that fuel these comparisons many times, every single day. We used to have so many distractions and buffers, in our lives as kids, that provided even the most insecure among us a cloak of emotional fuzziness. This blur slips into harsh, blunt focus for children now. It's right there, in their pocket, waiting to remind them that they are not good enough.

Consider the ideas that have historically made us insecure as adults. Our children are now aware of: the negative, upward comparisons to others; the idea that we may lack something important, or not have enough of it; the idea that we may be unloved or unlovable. These are now entering the consciousness of young children. And the thoughts on these topics are far from occasional, or even daily. Because of the nearly constant influx of stimuli in their lives, the traffic and noise in their very active minds, these thoughts play out nearly constantly for them.

And if these issues regularly create insecurity in us as adults, just imagine the impact they can have on the psyches of children, especially young children. And the imagery is relentless. They feel insecure virtually every day. It's pretty terrifying, for them and for us.

An Exercise in Self-Conscious Language

I encourage you to spend a day attending to your child, especially your young child, and the language they tend to use, especially regarding themself. Do you hear self-consciousness in their language? Do they reflect on how they look, or the nature of their personality, relative to others? Do they show signs of being self-deprecating, or insecure?

If they are beginning to show signs of self-consciousness in their thoughts and language, reflect aloud on your feelings about them. You've likely got a window here to guide them toward thinking more positively about themself. Show them the positive through your words, authentically (they will know if you are disingenuous). And model positive self-reflection in your own language about yourself. Through this exercise, you can help set them on a path toward positive self-regard.

Empathy

In the political swirl of recent years, our kids' generation has been labeled soft, coddled "snowflakes" who cannot handle and manage the realities of the "real world." They have been described as vapid, weak, self-involved people lacking true moral structure. Because they are so soft, sensitive, and self-involved, the narrative goes, they insist on gender-neutral bathrooms, safe spaces on campuses, and so on. And kids are aware enough, and well-read enough, to know that this is what we, generally, think of them.

This perception could not be further from the truth. These children have developed the ability to take on the perspective of others and, as a result, experience empathy without having to be lectured about it, as so many of us were. They feel abundant empathy, from a very early age, to the extent that they are emotionally overwhelmed. I believe kids feel more deeply now than they ever have, but their young minds are wholly unprepared for the broad perspective they have on the world, including the awareness of the suffering of others.

Kids today have an exceptionally high empathy load. If their friends are hurting, they are hurting. It's also important to remember that if *you* are hurting, they feel that as well. I don't know the parent who wants to pile their suffering onto their child, but your children are absorbing that nonetheless. It's important that you know that, along with their anxiety, your anxiety and fear is in their head as well.

Also, children today are far more open-minded, accepting of differences, and inclusive. They hold opinions on politics and culture. They are less likely to tolerate bullying or injustice of virtually any kind, and they recognize the emotional complexities not only of their own lives, but of the lives of others as well. This ability is creating a far more empathic generation, a generation far more engaged socially and politically than any generation preceding them. They feel deeply, not only their own joys, pains, and sorrows, but those of others as well, especially their peers. Too often, they serve as de facto therapists for one another, forgoing homework or sleep in favor of working through a friend's emotional difficulties. I have been told countless stories of suicidal teens claiming they would not be drawing breath were it not for a caring friend available to them in the middle of the night.

As a result, a striking number of kids say they want to do what I do as adults. They want to help others.

Of course, as much as this appears to be an encouraging phenomenon, it is challenging as well. I lean on five years of graduate school and endless hours of supervision to do this type of work effectively, and our kids are attempting to save the actual and emotional lives of their friends, on their own, often silently, with no training whatsoever. It can be an unreasonable, dangerous task for them to take on.

And I have worked with more than one child who served as a default counselor to a friend who has actually gone on to take his or her own life. And the ensuing guilt, that nagging question of whether he or she could have done something more to prevent the tragedy, does far more emotional damage than any child should ever have to bear.

You may wonder why our children talk to each other, especially when they feel emotions that may be life-threatening. I've asked a number of kids that very question, and the answers are unequivocal, and strikingly consistent. We parents are too often afraid of their fears, depression, and anxiety. Further, our kids are fully aware of our fear. So, they often go elsewhere. Shifting this dynamic is a crucial component of the parenting mandate here. Because children are not prepared to feel this degree of psychic pain, nor are they prepared to guide one another through it. So, we need to allay our own fears in order to be fully available to our children when they are in the fog or darkness of anxiety and depression.

When we feel that inclination to shrink away from our child, or that draw toward anger because they are presenting us with some powerful negative emotion we feel we cannot control, we need to turn directly toward them. We need them to know they can come to us when they feel their worst.

Social Media

Though I do not blame social media for all of the difficulties our children are suffering through, it does provide a frighteningly consistent set of comparison points for our newly self-conscious kids:

"She's better looking than I am."

"He's built better than me."

"She's way more popular than me—look at all those followers and likes."

"He has no acne, and I'm covered in it."

"She's so much skinnier than I am."

"He gets so many more girls than me."

For just a moment, picture the scene: Your child is alone in her room, silent, door closed. She is shut off from the world, alone with her social media. She reviews Instagram, and sees other girls posting photos (typically carefully selected from perhaps hundreds of selfies) doctored in the extreme, every blemish removed, every unwanted ounce erased, hair treated and digitally dyed, the posts accumulating likes as she watches. Your child looks on in a state of constant comparison, self-esteem bruised.

She switches to Snapchat, another widely-used social media platform. There, she may see group chats that exclude her, Snap streaks (consecutive days in communication with another user) broken, or friends at a party she either was never invited to, or was lied to by a friend about attending. And right before her is photographic evidence, not only that it is taking place, typically in real time, but also that it is awesome (for who among us presents our lonely, homely, broken moments on social media?).

In the past, we may have suspected that other people were deemed more popular than we were, or better looking, or were included socially on a more regular basis. Kids today—they *know*. They can see it, as they sit there alone, in their rooms, wondering why they were the ones excluded. And trust me here, many, many kids feel as if they have been singled out and left out. And they feel as if they are the only ones. This I hear an awful lot as well.

And here's where it gets even trickier. I worked with a sixteen-year-old girl, Christine, a while back who demonstrated for me how she crafted her daily selfie Instagram post. First, she would take hundreds of photos from various angles, trying to capture the cutest, brightest, thinnest, most perfect shot. Then, she would get to work editing the photo as described above. All told, Christine informed me that the process took, on average, about an hour a day.

During one session, she showed me her photo from the day before. She said, "Cute, right? I know, it actually looks nothing at all like me." Then she added, "But look at all the likes!"

Imagine the dissonance here: I take hundreds of selfies in order to find one that is workable, that makes me look physically acceptable. Then, I will change virtually every element of the pic, until I am nearly unrecognizable as myself. Only then am I willing to post my imposter image in order to gain likes, the slimmest of substitutes for self-worth.

And Christine is smart. She knows she is fooling herself. She's receiving the likes, but she is keenly aware that she has effectively manufactured something to attain them. It's a pretty empty win. But it works like an addiction. She feels as if she needs the likes, that they define an important part of her. Without them, she fears she would feel even worse about herself.

"This doesn't really represent me, but I'll be making another post like this tomorrow."

Teenagers fall into these daily loops easily, as posts and likes quickly become primary components of their sense of self-worth. And on Snapchat, for instance, the loops are encouraged, as kids work to sustain Snap streaks, in which they send and receive daily strings of messages to and from the same people. I have seen teenagers in tears when their phones are taken away as part of a punishment for some behavior or another. Often, the fear is that their Snap streaks will be broken, and their friends will have perpetuated longer streaks with other friends, making them less relevant, literally out of the social game. Even one day off breaks a streak, and can truly feel socially devastating. This all sounds absolutely ridiculous, I know.

But remember: your child did not come up with any of this, and as far as she is concerned, it has always been this way.

Herein lies a big part of the problem social media presents to our teens. Too often, they open their account with little self-worth, that sense of self-consciousness and negative comparisons to others striking them early in their lives. Social media being such a potent part of the currency of adolescence, and so critical to connection with peers, it's all but necessary for a thriving social life. But there is a massive layer of demand presented to kids as well. They not only feel the need to be "on" when they are at school or out with friends, but even when they are alone, during what once was downtime for children, they are working through their alternate identity, the one they are crafting on social media.

And make no mistake, social media is an enormous component of social currency, now and for the foreseeable future. And it is a craft. Have a look at your son or daughter's Instagram feed, their most recent Snap story. I suspect it is artful, or funny, or clever, or beautiful. Your kids work on this. For many, it is their primary method for bolstering their self-esteem, for forming an identity. Given that this is the first generation presented with this pressure-filled mandate, it's worthwhile to take a moment and marvel at what they have created out of the blank slate of an empty profile. They didn't come up with this—it has been foisted upon them. We owe them a moment of credit for what they do there.

Social media has rapidly become integral to teenage identity and self-worth. We don't have to appreciate this reality, but we do need to recognize and accept it.

There is another dark, insidious reality to social media. Bullying has become more of an online activity than a physical one. I have worked with so many teenagers who have had to see hate posts, and hate pages, put up online about them, for either all the world to see or, at the very least, their entire class. In part because they are created online, the assaults are more vicious and intense, the hate and berating more unbearable, than a physical confrontation in a school hallway could ever be. Cowardice works that way; it's the road rage of the internet. And like everything else posted "out there," the bullied teen can, and often does, revisit that awful page over and over again.

The bullied child will often tell me and their parents that it is no big deal, it's just playful, or it really doesn't hurt that much. But the pain is too palpable to ignore. If you find there is a bullying page or post about your child, it is time to advocate hard for her. Get on the phone with other parents. Call the school. Let it be known that this behavior will not be tolerated. I will warn you that your child will try to talk you out of this, suggesting that calling attention to the bullying will only make it worse. But that tends not to be the case in reality. Once called out, bullies tend to back down, especially if a grounding, suspension, or even expulsion lies in the balance. Having worked with bullies, I find they also feel a deep sense of shame and regret once exposed to the light of day. Bullying is more a projection of self-disdain than it is loathing for a classmate.

In fact, we need to pause and note here that bullying, online or otherwise, is never a one-dimensional issue. Part of the problem we have culturally is labeling without understanding, and *bully* is a heavy label. I have worked with many bullies in my career. And each time, I realize quickly that, though bullying may well be a behavior this child manifests, there are emotional reasons underlying their negative and hostile actions. More often than not, I find that, some time in their lives, bullies have been bullied, by a peer, a parent, or some other trusted adult in their lives. I find that bullies are, right under the arrogant and angry surface, deeply insecure, often lashing out before they can be victimized themselves. In order to evoke change culturally, we need to understand the pain of the bully as well as that of the bullied, and make sure that both receive the help they need to heal and move on. If we tend only to the bullied, we may unwittingly be perpetuating a cycle that can last for generations.

Keep this in mind if your child is accused of bullying of any kind. This behavior is unacceptable and damaging, but it is also, in its own way, a cry for help. Part of your mandate as a parent is to answer that cry. Make sure your child receives the help she needs, and please do not shy away from seeking professional help for your child. I cannot think of many circumstances under which this is a bad idea.

Okay, back to social media.

On the whole, I find that social media is too often a primary source of conflict between parents and children. And I get it—it is maddening to see your child, face down, constantly illuminated by the glow of their phone screen. But we need to keep in mind the meaning held in that screen for them.

And we need to present them with options. This is among the most important tasks parents need to face. I am often asked to provide a number: how much time per day is acceptable on social media?

It's a fair question, but it's the wrong question. More on this later.

Now, to be fair, many young people have offered me a very reasoned counterpoint to the scourge of screens and social media, a marked upside.

I was musing recently with a teenage client, Thomas, playing with the idea often spouted by my generation and the generation preceding me that kids today, through the shorthand of texting, emojis, memes, and flat-out stupid communication through Snapchat, are bastardizing and ruining the language.

"Kids can't write, or read, anymore," "The art of intelligent discourse is dead," I hear frequently. My wise young client Thomas pushed back hard on this notion, suggesting that quite the opposite is true. He pointed out, accurately, that his generation is actually very well-read and well-informed. Along with many of his contemporaries, he noted that his generation reads all the time, and is learning to be far more discerning and critical of what they ingest through all the internet has to offer.

"On our phones, we read way more than you guys did when you were our age, no doubt."

Fair enough, Thomas.

He cited, in particular, Reddit, an online clearinghouse of news digests, memes, jokes, and debates. Picture a Huffington Post for young people. It can be vulgar and offensive at times (that's part of the point), but it can be thought-provoking and highly informative as well. Twitter is another of his "news" sources, though with both sites, he does feel the need to dig in and verify information before developing an opinion.

So, Thomas would argue that his generation reads an incalculable number of pages of information per day, and is discerning truth and developing points of view nearly constantly, in real time. Unlike our generation, he would argue, they think in sophisticated ways all the time, every day. That discernment of thought may not be measured by exams in an English class, but Thomas does argue that it is a life skill his generation is the first to master at an early age, and which, in the internet age, will prove to be even more critical as time goes on.

Thomas would agree, by the way, that he and his friends communicate frequently via text shorthand, meme, or emoji. But he would further argue that older generations are missing the point. There is an understanding between young people that these methods are foolish and inane at times, but that is part of the humor in communicating that way. He adds that, "Well, at the very least, we are communicating, way, way more than your generation. We are in nearly constant touch with each other. So, if you guys are worried that we are socially out of touch, I think you're 100 percent wrong."

With smartphones, and the social and other media that accompany them, our kids discern more and think more than we ever did at their ages. We would do well to recognize, and find new ways to value, this fresh set of skills our kids are developing.

I also think we need to integrate some of them into our middle school and high school curriculum, by the way. I worked with Nathan, a bright, out-of-the-box-thinking nineteen-year-old, as he reflected on his high school years. Between sessions of taping a podcast with him, he offered the following wisdom:

"I can't believe we are still working with this outdated method of teaching, with textbooks and lectures, man! And the exams and papers, all the ways we measure what we've learned, it all needs to change. I mean, the reality is we *do* have the internet, and we *do* have brains. And these are the things we are going to use every day for the rest of our lives to distill information. But school systems work the same way they did fifty years ago, when none of this even existed. They've got to change with the times. Because I know a lot of brilliant kids. But that genius isn't gonna show up on a report card anymore."

You may not agree, but he's got both a point, and a point of view, right?

I have noted some other interesting forms of backlash to the onslaught among a select few young people. I have worked with several teenagers who, for various behavioral or emotional health-based reasons, have been sent by their families to therapeutic wilderness camps. I am quite fond of these settings, not only for the intensive individual and group therapy they provide, but also for taking troubled kids entirely out of their unhealthy context, providing them an immediate, far healthier geographic setting in which to heal. Set in beautiful outdoor locations, these camps are fully outdoors, and campers are, often for the first time in the lives, responsible for themselves and each other for food, shelter, warmth, and travel on foot from one site to the next for approximately two full months, sometimes longer.

And at camp, technology is strictly off limits.

The transition tends to be trying at first, as most kids are angry at their families for sending them, worried they will be left behind socially, and reset, hard, from all of their vices, including their iPhones (and vapes, Juuls, computers, iPads, weed, alcohol, processed foods, and so on). After that period of adjustment, though, there tends to follow several weeks of profound healing and change. Imagine how liberating it must feel to truly be away from all the tech that clouds our minds. Kids tell me they are firmly set in the present moment, focused

on the hike, or the river, or the sky, or their own breath. It's
a feeling most kids have likely never felt, and I suspect this
condition will only worsen with each passing year. Honestly,
I wish every kid could spare a couple of months out of their
adolescence to be a part of a camp atmosphere like this. How
cleansing for the body, mind, and spirit.

So, after the two months expire, kids return home. One boy told
me about a moment, just hours after leaving his camp, in which
he was in the front of a line at a McDonald's in the airport
nearby, heading home. He was looking at the menu when the
kid behind the counter yelled at him, "Come on already! What
do you want?"

"I don't know yet. I'm just looking."

Disgusted, the boy at the cash register yelled, "Next!"

"I just wasn't thinking at that pace anymore," my client told me.
"And I didn't want to."

He had learned a lot about himself while away. And one of the
first things he did was get rid of his smartphone, in favor of a
retro flip phone. He knew he would want the ability to text his
friends once he fully reintegrated into his life back home, but
he also knew the smartphone was inherently toxic to his well-
being, and he felt he was fully addicted to it before camp.

He is far happier now, and feels more emotionally in-balance
than ever before. He never knew the type of peace of mind he
experienced at camp was possible. It had never occurred to him,
as he had never known a world without fairly constant access
to a "soul-sucking" screen. A couple other clients of mine have

followed suit, returning from a therapeutic wilderness camp and forgoing the smartphone, at least for a time. A couple of others, who have kept their phones, take breaks from social media, removing the apps from their phones in order to clear their minds. One girl in particular replaces Snapchat with Headspace, a simple and elegant meditation app, for a week or so every couple of months. She finds emotional self-regulation and balance that way.

My hope for our children is that we are quickly reaching critical mass, and a backlash is imminent. I suspect this generation will overtly begin to recognize the number their black mirrors are doing on their minds and their well-being, and seek wellness and balance instead. This is a thoughtful and intelligent group, this generation. They are better poised than any of us to make such a change.

In the meantime, I think we parents can do a couple of things to foster that change, and hasten it a bit. First, we of course need to better regulate our own screen time, including our time spent on social media. Modeling the behavior we want to encourage is the most effective method, and I think we are inherently aware of this reality. We can also take screen breaks as a family, and find some other activity to engage in collectively. And finally, I would strongly encourage you not to jump the gun in terms of providing your child with an iPhone or iPad. Wait a year or two. Allow them the space to breathe in the world with their eyes up, free of the overstimulation of the screen. I find that the more practice a client of mine has at this, the less likely they are to impulsively reach for their phone immediately as it buzzes, summoning their attention in the middle of a session.

Finally, I have worked with many parents who feel as if they no longer really know their teenager, this child they ushered into the world, who, up until just a few years ago, trusted them with almost everything, social, academic, or emotional. Now, they are upstairs behind a closed door, and they feel shut out of their world. I find, more and more, that the parents I learn are snooping in their child's room, or on their various social media accounts, are not necessarily trying to "catch" their child in some misdeed. No, fundamentally, I have learned that an awful lot of parents *miss* their teenagers, and want to be part of their worlds again. Social media, even a "Finsta," can be an interesting reintroduction to your child.

A Finsta (short for a fake Instagram account), for those of you who may be unfamiliar, is the second Instagram account your child may not tell you about, the one she shares with a select group of friends. That Finsta may prove more racy, salacious or, at times, inappropriate than what you are invited to see. Just know that, on any social media platform, your child may very well have more than one account, with split identities to keep track of. I find that this stuff gets very complicated when you really dig into it with teenagers. I feel for them that they sense a need to navigate it all, keep all those identity plates spinning every day, in order to just tread water socially.

A lot of the kids I work with invite me to follow them on some social media account or another. I find what I see there to be, on the whole, quite revealing: heartening, funny, sweet, and occasionally inappropriate, as teenagers are wont to be. But it's so good to know them in this way, and sometimes talents and interests become apparent in a way that discussion does not always foster. I have discovered I am sitting across from a budding photographer, or a musician, or an artist, from clients' social media. So, for parents, I encourage you not to fight the trend. It's a very important part of the life of a child, understandably. And it's a fight you will lose regardless. Instead, I encourage you to join in. Ask your child if you can follow her. You will feel closer to her. It's pretty cool.

And remember, again, none of this is your child's idea. As far as she is concerned, it has always been this way.

Defusing the Power of FOMO

FOMO, or the Fear of Missing Out, has become a far more impactful phenomenon in the age of social media, and the concomitant increase in social anxiety. I find that many parents find themselves inclined to reason their child through their FOMO: "You really couldn't possibly be missing out on anything *that* important" or "Get your work done more efficiently, and you will have more time to spend with your friends." I totally understand these tactics, and the fairly sound reasoning underlying them.

But FOMO tends to be a highly emotional and anxiety-inducing experience for a lot of kids, and reasoning through it does precious little to ease a teen's anxiety. Instead, I would encourage you to think about your own experience of FOMO, as a teenager or, as so many of us experience, in the present day. Share your experiences with your child. Let them know you can relate to their feelings, and acknowledge the reality that they may well be missing out on something that might matter to them socially. This degree of understanding alone may ease some of their anxiety, just the knowing that someone "gets it."

Then, I think it makes sense to work through the logistics with them: "You are probably going to miss out on something on occasion—we all do. But that's okay. Most of us are trying to balance our work, other obligations, and social life. And, big picture, things tend to work out the way they need to." Then, "How can we get you more involved socially?"

And please, if you feel you're over your parental skis here, consult with a professional. The social anxiety affiliated with a persistent fear of missing out often requires therapy to rejuvenate a sense of self-worth, and perhaps some social skills training to get them connecting with peers. This really is that important.

With this exercise, you accomplish a couple of things: You let your child know you understand their FOMO, and that you have experienced that feeling yourself. You also get them involved in problem-solving their FOMO instead of feeling distracted, anxious, and upset about it.

Antidotes to Social Media

In this age of social media overload, we need to step back and consider how our children spend their time, and the activities and outlets available to them to develop both a sense of self, and a sense of self-worth. We need to provide them with multiple avenues through which to do so, especially given the magnetic pull of social media. So, this is the area of parenting in which I most strongly encourage you to play the "parent card." If your child seems disengaged outside of social media, or video games, or some other screen-based activities, press them to get involved. Fill the bulk of their time with school, sports, groups, plays, music, or clubs. Get them moving their bodies, something teenagers today do less and less.

Physical activity is something they desperately need.

My take on this has changed quite a bit. Years ago, I encouraged young people to think more. Now, so many kids spend far too much of their time lost in thought loops, many of them maladaptive and overly self-deprecating. Today, they need to spend far less time lost in thought, and more time doing. It is in the actual doing—the running, swimming, acting, singing, dancing, talking, and laughing—that a deeper sense of identity can be found, more tangible and true. It is in doing that our kids can prove to themselves that they are smart and capable and competent and resilient.

Perhaps the most critical component of doing, one that is missed by this entire generation, lies in moving one's body. Due in large part to the draw of the various screens our children access, the natural inclination to move, run, swim, and sweat is derailed, often entirely. The result is a passive generation, running and jumping in video games, or momentarily playing for videos to post on one social media platform or another. As a result, we are raising ever more sedentary children, who are more obese than ever and holding more anxiety in their physical bodies. And I find that movement is the single most potent reliever of pent-up anxiety, period.

Young bodies want to move, to run and swim and dance and play. Too many kids decide they are not athletes, far too early in life to make that determination. Too many parents support that assertion, and fail to encourage movement. Here is a script worth changing.

Because, without some press from us, our kids are simply not presented with enough impetus to move. All their lives, there has been a screen that provided ample entertainment, and many kids have never gained an alternative, consistent point of view. It is our job as parents to present them with these options; thus the critical importance of the "parent card."

I read recently about the decline in attendance at summer camps, both sleepaway camps and day camps. My experience with my client base over the years supports this trend. And for those of you with younger children, I strongly urge you to consider having your child attend a summer camp. Make it a part of the fabric of your family, an expectation. There are countless benefits to camps, as there have always been: introductions to new friends, sports, music, and other activities, to be sure. But today, the benefits are invaluable. Your child will spend a week or two or more, or several hours a day, engaged in other activities besides the phone. Over time, even kids who are quite reluctant to attend camps tend to rise to the occasion, and enjoy participating. I personally find that kids who attend camps tend to carry that balance with them long after camp is completed, spending more time outdoors, playing, laughing, making up games, and being fully engaged with friends.

Spending some time engaged in volunteer activity can also provide this balance. Once you play your "parent card" here, you will find, I predict, that your child's volunteer participation becomes somewhat self-sustaining. Not only does it bring balance to be free of social media and other social pressures, as well as academic and perhaps familial stressors, but your child will also, in all likelihood, discover how much she enjoys being of service to others. Kids frequently describe to me how invaluable their time serving others can be to them, how important it is to see the faces of the people they are helping, and how grateful they become for their own life circumstances. Volunteer work pays countless dividends. Again, I encourage you to make service an automatic part of the family creed. It is tough to get your teenager out there if volunteering and service are not already a core part of the vernacular. It can be done with a "parent card," of course, but if you have younger children, get them serving others early.

Self-Reflection, Self-Control, and Social Media

Research shows that we adults grossly underestimate the time we spend daily on social media, often by a factor of hours. I encourage you to track an average day, and honestly look at your track record. Do you spend an hour on social media? Two? More? The answer is yes for many of us. I find that once we are aware, truly and fully aware, of the amount of time we spend, and waste, on social media every single day, we are far more inclined to change the habit.

One of the best ways to reset your social media habit, as a family, is to pick a day—I find a Sunday works best—and fully fast from social media. All phones and computers and pads are off for twenty-four hours. You will hear grousing and complaining. You may even be the one complaining most. But when the fog clears, you will find yourself, your children, your entire family, are far more present in the moment with one another. This exercise will remind you, and perhaps teach your kids for the first time, that most of the good things in life take place away from the screens. A day off, heading into the city or out to the country on a family adventure, will punctuate that point nicely.

You may have to mandate this exercise to get it to actually happen, but it will be well worth it.

The Emotional Bank Account

Many parents have told me they do not feel as if they have a "parent card" to play. They are certain their child would not sign up for a sport, play, or club, even if they insisted upon it. Their child will not listen and will not comply. And the pull of the screen feels far more potent than any parenting power we may have felt we could exert in the past.

This is where the Emotional Bank Account comes into play. This account is among my favorite methods for examining any relationship. If you read my first book, or if you have ever heard me speak publicly, you will find yourself quite familiar with this crucial concept which is a key to effective parenting.

The balance in the Emotional Bank Account, or EBA, is effectively an indication of the accumulated goodwill in any relationship. If things are running smoothly and your relationship feels resilient to any minor difficulties or bumps in the road you may encounter together, you are looking at an EBA that is solidly in the black. If, however, you feel disconnected and that communication is either one-way or trying, if either or both of you feel unheard or misunderstood, the EBA is likely in the red. This is a relationship that is in trouble and, in all likelihood, causes significant emotional distress, conflict, and a sense of disconnection for both parties.

The very good news here is that the EBA is flexible, pliable, and forgiving. The balance can be shifted with any deposit or withdrawal. Anything smacking of a disconnect will read as a withdrawal: an inopportune judgment, a lengthy lecture, or a misplaced punishment, for example. These may feel like good ideas, and perhaps even parenting mandates, in real time. But with the culture shifting so dramatically and rapidly, we need to be operating from a new parenting playbook, one in which we will frequently need to call real-time parenting audibles based on the needs of our child and our connection with our child. Today, we simply cannot afford unnecessary withdrawals from the EBA. A positive balance here trumps nearly every other factor in parenting.

Because if we are parenting from an EBA in the red, our voice is unheard, and our parenting is frustratingly ineffective. All of this can be quite frightening at times like these, when we know how critical our input is for the well-being of our children.

So, how then do we deposit into the EBA? How do we sustain a balance well in the black?

This is the good news, and perhaps the best, most enjoyable part of parenting. To increase the balance in the EBA, we simply connect. We table the lecture, and we play with our kids. We laugh with them. We create in-jokes with them. We dig in and learn all we can about their worlds: the music they listen to, the video games they play, the social media they favor, the teams they follow, their politics, and so on. And listen *with* them, play *with* them, cheer *with* them. Dig in without judgment, and with true curiosity, and you will find yourself well on your way to a smoother connection, an EBA in the black. But if you are hunting for trouble under the guise of connecting, if you are looking for clues as to how your child is performing in class, or whether she is hanging out with the wrong crowd or posting something inappropriate, your child will sense the disingenuous gesture. There will be a time for all of that if you sense that your child's well-being, health, or safety is in jeopardy.

But to build the EBA—especially one in which the balance is already fractured—work on the connection. If you feel your child is a stranger to you, they feel the same. Rediscover your connection. It was there once, not that long ago. And from our parental perspective, we tend to disconnect from a place of fear—fear that if we do not bear down and control our child, he or she will wind up in peril.

But the logic here is faulty. It is precisely that connection itself, that positive balance in the EBA, that effectively inoculates our child from such peril. With so many elements of her life drawing down her sense of self-worth, your Unconditional Positive Regard will prove to be the godsend that will provide a crucial layer of protection from the dangers you fear for her. So, it is urgent that you see past your fear in order to recognize where the value in your relationship lies.

She does not need your lecture. She already knows how you feel. Just ask her. She does not need your judgment. She is highly self-aware, and likely over-judging herself. She does not need your ire or unkindness. Her world is harsh enough as it is. Rather, she needs your light. She needs to know that, despite anything she feels about herself, anything she may do incorrectly, and any poor choices she makes, you are there for her, 100 percent, unconditionally. Your relationship with her can be her port in the storm of adolescence. In my opinion, that's the best parenting story you can possibly write.

An Emotional Bank Account Inventory

Both Daniel Goleman, the author of *Emotional Intelligence*, and Dr. John Gottman, a prominent expert on relationships, have discussed the ratio of positive to negative interactions necessary to maintain a good working relationship. Though they reflect primarily on intimate relationships, I find that their work applies equally well to the parent-child relationship.

And the ratio required to maintain and sustain a positive balance in the EBA is five to one, five positive interactions for every negative interaction. This finding shows us the powerful impact a single negative interaction can have on a relationship, and how much positive interaction is required to balance it out.

Consider for a moment your relationship with your child. For a day or two, keep track of the interactions you share, and create an honest accounting of net positive and net negative interactions. If you find (as most parents I have coached through this exercise have) that you are nowhere near that ratio, create more positive interactions with your child. Talk about interests, common or otherwise. Focus on something other than the homework she is supposed to be doing, or the dishwasher that needs emptying, or the attitude she's been showing lately. Because this research is powerful and holds true. If you lack abundant positive interaction with your child, your influence in her life will be greatly diminished, increasing your frustration with parenting and driving a deeper wedge between you both emotionally.

This is among the most important exercises you can engage in as a parent.

About Your Disdain

Okay, this might sound harsh, but it's important. To your child, your fear and judgment may look like disdain. She cannot bear the burden of your disdain.

Expectations, yes.

Disdain?

Well, that just may break her.

I bring the potential for parental disdain up for a reason. I see it, frequently. In therapy sessions, it is painfully clear and obvious when a parent is so baffled and upset by a child's shifting behavior and affect that they express disdain. I find that, upon a moment's inspection, that disdain is virtually always a reflection of fear and frustration on the part of the parent. Fear that we may be doing it all wrong, that we may not have any agency over our precious child. Frustration that they will not remain with the program, fall in line, and be better.

But this is a delicate issue, because what feels like fear and frustration to us falls like disdain on the senses of far too many of our children. And I can tell you, with an insider's perspective, that most children carry a rather persistent thought that they may not be good enough on their own. Piling a sense that you hold disdain for them on top of that is often more than a child can bear. This produces many of the symptoms of anxiety, depression, and other emotional suffering I see in practice.

So please be very aware of showing disdain for your child. Now more than ever, it is critical to parse the difference between character and behavior. That is, your child may, and likely will, exhibit behavior of which you disapprove, and you can speak your mind on that.

But it is far more important that your child hears from you, and sees in the way you present to her, that she is fundamentally *good*, and good enough, regardless of what she may be doing in the moment.

So, at the very least, your children need your empathy. They need to know that you are available to them, free of fear and judgment and ego. They need to know that you see them and that you *feel* them. And in order to feel them, to truly experience empathy for your children, it is incumbent upon you to show that you understand them, that you are willing to step into their worlds.

This precept is one of those ideals that seem simple, but believe me, it can be very, very difficult. Because your child may very well be experiencing the very darkest of feelings and emotions, even if she offers a palatable and pleasant face to the rest of the world. I bear witness to this jarring paradox many times a week. Clinically, this mismatch between expressed and felt emotion can be a dangerous, even lethal emotional brew. For now, it is far more difficult to tell, on the face of things, whether your child is "okay" than it used to be. I have preached in the past that simply asking suffices and lets your child know you are available and in their corner.

But at eight, nine, ten, or eleven years old or older, we cannot expect our children to possess the insight to know whether they are "okay," or even what "okay" looks and feels like. For the emotional dissonance they are experiencing may be the only state of being they have ever consciously known, and the "okay" label carries no more meaning than any other would.

So, we need to find empathy, with some degree of urgency. To do so, we need to be willing to hear the worst from our kids. And, in my experience, the darkest thoughts imaginable often haunt their young minds. For instance, in the past few years, I have heard the following from children as young as eight or nine:

"I hate the way I look."

"I hate who I am."

"I am a toxic person."

"Everyone would be far better off without me."

By far the most common negative sentiment I hear, on a *very* regular basis, goes something like this:

"I am not going to kill myself, but if I do not wake up tomorrow morning, that's fine by me. In fact, that would be ideal."

I had rarely heard this passive suicidality until about five years ago, but now it feels ubiquitous among young people. When I press them on it, I find that this is not a wish to die, but for internal suffering to end. It is critical to note that the management of their own internal anxieties and shifting emotions has become a primary task for children and is inextricably tied to identity development. This is a new challenge for our kids, one we need to be available to take on with them.

For children today hold themselves to impossibly high standards, the fallout being an almost inevitable feeling of not being good enough. For one, they consistently feel as if they must possess clarity of purpose, life purpose, sometimes before puberty even fully settles in. In their minds, they are failing and feel quite lost, if they fail to attain this. More on this as we move forward.

For now, please keep this parental mandate, this mandate free of disdain, fear, judgment, and ego, in mind as we begin to tackle the individual issues you will be facing as parents one by one.

Identity Traffic

I was talking with a brilliant fifteen-year-old girl, Katie, the other day about the changing nature of identity in her generation. She laughed when I asked her how she felt she and her peers defined "identity," because it suggests we have only one.

"You must mean *identities*, Dr. Duffy!"

Katie used herself as an example in explaining what she meant. There was the identity she presented to friends. This comprised thoughtfulness, being fun and funny, and availability to help with any of their problems, among other things. She then talked about the identity she presented to her parents and family, one in which she was obedient and studious and upbeat and more interested in school than in social media and boys. She followed that up with her identity on social media, the über-popular, cute, clever, effortlessly awesome party girl with thousands of likes, literally.

Katie mentioned other identities she feels she needs to maintain as well. She has a different identity with boys than with girls. She feels she needs to act differently when in the company of different cliques, whether she feels she is a part of these groups or not. She needs to be pert and perfect with the popular kids, dark and pensive with her emo friends, and driven and strong on her soccer team. She carries different identities and presentations for teachers, coaches, and her boss.

Finally, Katie talked about who she really felt she was, deep down inside. She suggested this identity scared her the most, because it was real and not constructed. She had no control over the "real" Katie. She was dark and moody sometimes, and hated herself at times as well. She saw through her "bullshit" to the true and empty essence of all these phony, plastic identities she presented to the world.

To avoid the real Katie, as she called her, she would listen to music on Spotify, or watch reruns of *The Office* or *Parks and Rec* until she was too tired to stay awake, and the real Katie would leave her be.

I think Katie speaks for an awful lot of her peers when she describes this identity confusion, which she brilliantly labeled *identity traffic*. No wonder kids today feel less equipped to determine who they are and the roles they want to play in the world. With all this noise playing in their minds, all this identity traffic, it is not only difficult but, as Katie suggests, not always very desirable, to hear your own voice, your authentic self, from deep inside. For that voice may be calling you out as a fraud more than she is supportive and loving. She may be a brutal truth-teller. And hiding underneath other identities may appear more bearable.

As Katie suggested, teenagers today are therefore never truly free from anxiety. Time on your phone, and engaged in social media, is anxiety-provoking. And time away from your phone, at school, at parties, doing homework, or with your family, can all be anxiety-inducing as well. Kids today are never truly off the grid, free to hear themselves think. In their minds, they are rarely, if ever, truly free. Managing identity traffic is more than a full-time job.

So here lies another particular parenting challenge. What you think is on your child's mind, or ought to be on her mind, is often on the back burner: the grades, the job, the ACT scores, the extracurricular activities. The prevailing fog in the forefront of her mind reverberates with the nagging question: who am I?

How do we guide our kids in navigating all of these different identities? The first thing we need to keep in mind is that she needs to hear a lot of her own voice and not so much of yours.

So, you ask a lot of open questions. In my practice, I find curiosity to be the most effective tool for navigating the traffic. I have learned that kids know who they are, but they rarely experience that moment outside the identity traffic to calmly, quietly consider themselves. You do not, therefore, need to talk them into feeling better about themselves. You also do not need to delineate their résumé to them, or a list of their relative strengths. I find that this approach creates more identity traffic for them, not less.

Instead, ask calmly and curiously what it is like for her to carry, manage, and navigate through these different identities. Ask which feels most authentic to her, and which feels most artificial. She may tell you that, when you peel away all the "false selves," she does not like herself much. You will likely hear that she feels lonely a lot of the time, even when she is with people, and particularly when she is on social media. You may hear that she does not value herself, or even her life, to a great extent. You want to be a safe, reliable holding place for these emotions. This space is so curative for the incessant identity traffic kids suffer. I find it to be invaluable and essential to a child's sense of well-being.

And remember, in all of these conversations, to table your judgment. After all, none of this was your child's idea. And, as far as she is concerned, it has always been this way.

I pass a grammar school on the way to work. On the first day of school, I stopped and watched the commotion. I watched smiling parents, iPhones up, recording the firsts: walking to school, getting in line, walking in. I watched as parents cajoled their kids for reactions to the camera, either for a well-rehearsed mugging smile or a "Dad, I'm fed up with this" face.

I experienced a couple of profound reactions that morning. First, I recognized that those kids had been looking at the backs of phones, their every move recorded, for years. And I get it. I did it with my son as well. We want to capture moments. But, in doing so, we cannot deny that we miss them. We also cannot deny that we alter them, interfere with them, by jumping in with the recorder. The moment loses its organic nature. It becomes a photo op. And far too many moments in our kids' young lives become photo ops. It limits the joy of the moment, but it also subconsciously plants the seeds of their future online personas, those very identities we parents will be frustrated with just a few years on. There's a better, more balanced way here, and I think we are all aware of that fact, and where the mandate for change falls.

It's on us.

In that moment, the phone also creates a breach between parent and child. They were not meeting eye-to-eye, but eye-to-lens. Consider for a moment how odd this must be for a child. They lose a critical element of connection with Mom and Dad, at crucial ongoing developmental periods of their lives, at important moments. They are not seeing eyes. And eye contact is so important to connection. We become anxious when we do not feel seen. We feel this as adults. Just imagine what it must be like for children. No wonder this generation is experiencing more anxiety than any other. Our kids need that direct connection with us, free of the barrier of the camera.

The New Late Teen

On the back end of adolescence, biology and culture also provided parents some guidance in the past. Typically, a generation ago or further back, young adults were off to college, junior college, or a career in a trade by nineteen. Most had experienced enough independence to tend to their well-being outside the home, and, somewhere between eighteen and twenty, they took the first steps toward independent living. That is to suggest that, in the past, the end of adolescence presented a fairly predictable arc, with an equally predictable beginning, middle, and end. Those who veered off course in one way or another were fairly easily identified. And again, course correction was often initiated by the cadre of adults surrounding the late adolescent.

The story plays out very differently today. Now, young people are inundated with so much data, driving so much dissonance and identity traffic, that this process is winding and jagged, moving more in fits and starts than smoothly and gradually. So, adolescence tends to be prolonged on the back end, as young adults continue to navigate the persistent identity traffic that marks the teen years.

A significant contributor lies in the fact that, despite conventional wisdom, kids are literally thinking and considering their place in the world at earlier and earlier ages. Though this seems at the outset to be a positive shift, I find it can be quite overwhelming, and, beneath the harsh self-judgment of adolescence, it can spark identity confusion at every turn and, in many cases, a powerful sense of self-loathing. For many kids decide early on that they have far too little to contribute. They feel they should be further along in determining their identities and roles. And, just like that, an adolescence that was jump-started far too early is stalled on the back end, derailed by discouragement and uninspired direction.

Some of my clients well into their twenties feel stuck, dismayed that the linear progression they may have expected did not occur for them. They are troubled that they do not fit into the narrow definition of success we are all responsible for deriving and are working through not only issues of self-worth and self-esteem, but often despondency, anxiety, and depression. Too many of them find that there is so much they need to undo before they can get out in the world and do. I cannot express to you how discouraging this can be to these young adults: the self-judgment and self-loathing and fear. They suddenly, over the past several years, comprise far too great a percentage of my practice.

Of course, some teenagers and young adults do follow the prescribed linear progression and conform to that narrow definition of success. They work for the grades, take all the AP classes, sign up for the teams and clubs and groups. They select the right majors and study. Once out in the world, however, a number of young adults find themselves unfulfilled, feeling hoodwinked by the path they thought would bring "success," only to realize they weren't sure exactly which, and whose, definition of success they had been chasing their entire lives. The resulting depression and dismay this can cause in someone never given license to hear her own voice can be quite devastating, and it can take several years to recalibrate and find the more effective, happier path. So, even if a child follows the predictable linear progression, they far too often find the outcome to be empty and disappointing.

There is a rather stunning new phenomenon regarding college freshmen. We feel as if we prepare our teenagers so well for this time in their lives. They have managed their way through a challenging high school curriculum. We have taught them to cook, do laundry, and consider where on campus it will prove most effective to do their homework.

But here's the stark reality. A full 30 percent of college freshmen return home before Christmas at the end of their first collegiate semester, a majority of them young men. A study recently completed by the World Health Organization also found that a full third of college students suffer from a significant mental health condition. This is a somewhat hidden phenomenon, as these young people are not proud to be back home. They are invisible, sitting ashamed in basements, playing Fortnite, smoking weed, feigning job interviews to appease their parents, and trolling social media.

I have seen more than a dozen of these bewildered college freshmen in each of the past five or six years. The themes that brought them to my office are strikingly consistent. They drank too much, smoked too much, slept too much, or failed to go to class. Effectively, due to an excessively high level of anxiety, each of these young people had failed to self-regulate in significant ways that exerted profound negative effects on their levels of functioning.

Collectively, these young adults present a strong case for teaching emotional self-regulation before they head off to college or their next post-high-school adventure. And, if we are not teaching self-regulation through the schools, it is incumbent upon us as parents to instill these skills at home.

Otherwise, we are again prolonging the dependence and lack of clear personal identity that are the hallmarks of adolescence.

Many of those college students who remain on campus, by the way, are also suffering mental health issues, including significant depression and anxiety, as well. I conduct sessions with college students suffering on campus every academic year, and many therapists I know have substantial waiting lists for this population. I believe that, on the whole, we tend to underutilize the resources available to our young adults on campus. Most campuses, for instance, provide a Counseling and Psychological Services (CAPS) program, offering sessions to undergraduate and graduate students at very reasonable rates. Some of these are better staffed than others, so I encourage any new freshmen I know to set up a time with a therapist on campus soon after they arrive, so that they will have someone to go to, a professional familiar with their story, should they need help as the semester goes on.

We also do not make good use of tutorial and Individualized Education Plan (IEP) services offered on campus. I recently worked with a young woman who worked in the evenings at a tutoring program at the University of Iowa. She told me that students would rarely show up for help, though she knew many people could use it. She lamented that many of her fellow students were struggling unnecessarily, failing to use the tools that were at their disposal for free. I have also talked with professors and teaching assistants who have felt the same way, sitting on their own during office hours. I urge you to encourage your child to make full use of the resources available to her from as young an age as possible. It is a little-used life skill that serves us so well throughout our lives, if we are willing to avail ourselves of it.

Adolescence is prolonged today also because of what our children see taking place in the lives of the adults around them. It is neither particularly promising nor appealing to them. Their parents may seem unhappy, depressed, and harried, for instance. Yet they often encourage their children to follow the paths they followed. This prolongs the feeling of hopelessness many young people suffer, as they fear they will end up sad and uninspired, grinding through endless days filled with meaningless tasks. They fear they will not make a living, or, worse, they will never make a difference in the lives of others or in the world. So, they effectively freeze in place, holding onto adolescence in an effort to stave off a vast, foreboding, and unfulfilling adulthood.

I worked recently with Lauren, a brilliant young woman who set herself up beautifully for her adult life. She worked hard in high school, achieving nearly perfect grades, serving on the student council, and participating in multiple sports through the varsity level. As she had planned, she gained admission into several of the right schools and chose one. Shortly after arriving on campus, she recognized a deep disappointment in the lack of depth and meaning in her life. Emotionally, she shut down. She feels nothing, despite doing everything right, and she's terrified by that dearth of emotion. I worry about young adults like Lauren, as her level of functioning was, in most ways, unaffected by this emotional shift. She continued to go to class and master perfect grades. She doesn't present as either depressed or anxious. She feels completely flat affect-wise but can shift to bubbly and upbeat in a moment. In other words, nobody would know her level of despair and hopelessness, for now and for her future.

And the hard truth is, Lauren can't talk to her parents. Her home is silent. Her parents are remote to her, emotionally unavailable. And maybe they think everything's just fine. So, together, Lauren and I are working on finding what does make her feel, what does give her purpose, and life, and hope.

There are a lot of Laurens out there.

They feel no hope. They don't see their way to a fulfilling life in which they can make a contribution. They are locked into the narrow definition of success presented to them their entire lives, and cannot, on their own, identify another way through. We need to provide the Laurens of this world the space to hear their own voices. This girl is brilliant and kind. She needs the hope that comes with her voice. We have to recognize that we, collectively, need it as well.

So, just because your child is doing well "on paper" does not necessarily mean she's doing well. Don't make any assumptions about whether your child is fine, unless you have talked with her.

A recent study in *Child Development* offers another theory on the postponement of the end of adolescence and the onset of adulthood. The results of this research suggest that teenagers today participate in fewer "adult" activities, ostensibly due to arrested development driven by a fixation on smartphones and other similarly distracting devices. Specifically, this study points out that, over the course of the last twenty years, teenagers drink less alcohol, date less, have sex later and less frequently, spend less time with their parents, and drive less. On the other hand, they tend to be home more, including weekend evenings, and be alone more frequently, perhaps impeding their social development compared with previous generations. They remain emotionally unhealthy, regressed, and suppressed in teenage activity.

Many young adults feel as if they have already failed in their lives and that it is too late to change course now that they are nineteen, or twenty-one, or twenty-three. I work with more people suffering from depression and an overall sense of hopelessness in this age group now than I have in any of the past twenty-five years of practice, by a significant margin.

The answer here, as in so many instances, is to provide a modicum of hope to what feels hopeless. Much of the hopelessness I've come across is derivative of this "failure fallacy" detailed above: I have not figured out what to do with my life to date, so I have failed. A recent article in *Time* suggested that, though my generation was likely to engage in one or two careers in our lifetimes, this generation will have four to five career progressions, some of which may not yet exist. That is to say, a young adult today does not need to have a direct bead on what she wants to do career-wise for the rest of her life, not by a long shot. She just has to determine what she wants to do first, what she is inclined to do next. The idea that there are steps and progressions involved in one's career and in one's life is often very liberating, I have found. It can provide a broad window of hope for the young adult who is struggling to reason her way out of her current circumstances.

I recognize that, if you are in what feels like a hopeless situation with your young adult, this may be a lot to ask. Many people in their early twenties live at home, drink too much or smoke too much weed, play video games, and stare off into their phones. This presentation can make even the most cool-minded parent lose it. So, if you find yourself in these straits, draw in a few deep breaths and recognize that nobody *wants* to be listless, idle, and potentially self-medicating. Your child is likely in that spot for lack of clear direction and perhaps a fear of failing more, or again. We tend to opt out when we feel our odds of success are slim. So, you can spare your child and yourself the lectures about what they should be doing, as you, in all likelihood, find that approach to be tiresome and fruitless. Try the above approach instead. It will work far better, allow space for some traction and forward movement, and foster a collaborative environment in which you will be seen more as an ally, guide, and consultant, and less as an enemy to be avoided. Again, this is the best story you can write with your young adult child.

The Late Starter–A Success Story

I recently worked with a bright and likeable young man, Steven, who struggled in school but found his way stumbling toward an acceptable, traditional path. He gained access, barely, into what felt to his family like a reasonable university. He stumbled through freshman year, landing on academic probation and taking a year to regroup at a community college. He regained admission, barely, into the college he had left. And seemed back in business.

All along, he noted to both his parents and myself that he not only disliked school, but felt that something was missing and lacking in his life. He felt he was on the wrong track.

Still, he pressed on.

During one of our weekly Skype sessions, Steven asked about the trades: electricians, carpenters, plumbers, and so on. He wondered whether he could make a living in one of those careers. Once he realized this remained a viable path, he immediately brightened. I mean, in that very moment, he lit up. He decided he was in his very last college semester, and trade school and apprenticeship would be his next steps. He was psyched.

Other changes followed, changes none of us might have predicted. A prolific drinker, Steven chose a far more moderate route. Historically overweight, he also began to hit the gym and lost thirty pounds rather quickly, leaving a leaner, healthier, more muscular physique. He felt relief from the persistent anxiety he had suffered for years. Steven reported being far more honest with himself, his family, and his friends.

When I asked him what drove these changes, he said he felt as if he had found himself. He was proud and excited that he had a path he could feel good about.

He said he was the stereotypical late starter, and that he is forever grateful that his parents never gave up on him, even if they did not provide him with ready solutions over the years. So, if your child has not found her way yet, hang in with her. Be the patient parent that trusts their child's process and voice and competence and resilience. And that faith will carry her in the meantime.

Just as Steven's parents' faith carried him.

You may have seen a recent headline about a high school that held a signing day for graduating seniors celebrating, one by one, their exciting next steps in life. The cool thing about this signing day was that they were lauding young adults who were *not* going to college, but had jobs—in the trades, in factories, warehouses, stores, and family businesses. These remain viable, highly important paths as well, and we need to continue to honor and value them.

This is no small thing, as I find this young generation is more aware than any preceding them of the importance of making a contribution to society. We cannot narrow down the definition of success here either and need to value contributions from the most educated, to the hardest-working, to the most skilled. College is not required, nor is it for everyone. I applaud any young person who recognizes that it is not for them or, at the very least, not for them right now.

Now, some of these young men and women will go to college one day, perhaps when they feel the time is right. Others will certainly enjoy flourishing careers in jobs that many of us will need them for ad infinitum. Let's not diminish their accomplishments or the critical roles they play in our society.

Our Narrow Definition of Success

As I've suggested a number of times, our changing, narrowing definition of success is a significant contributor to the Age of Anxiety, as well as the identity traffic our kids suffer. Most every subject discussed thus far can be looked at as a standalone behavior to be parented, managed, and mitigated. Or, peeling back one additional layer of depth, each can be seen as a symptom of a greater cultural issue, a method for coping with an ever-more-stressful world.

There is good news here for us parents: part of this anxiety is within our locus of control, if we are willing to recognize it. We have collectively come up with a very slim definition of success, of acceptable behavior and outcomes. Much of what we have chosen as part of this definition is objective: you need to achieve this grade, get into this school, make this team, play this chair in orchestra. Our own anxiety has us pressing an agenda on our kids very early. They need to achieve in a very linear sense. They need to meet certain benchmarks in terms of GPA, ACT scores, number of extracurricular activities, and so on. We are working, of course, from the very best of intentions, we tell ourselves. Because our children either cannot or will not, we are playing the long game for them.

And if we reflect for a moment, the long game has to do, in large part, with the tier of college our child attends. As parents, we want them to do the very best they can performance-wise, so that opportunities remain open to them.

The problem, of course, is that this game does not allow much for individuality. It folds our kids into a very small box that allows precious little space for play, experimentation, and thriving. It does nothing for the self-esteem of the child who is creative, artistic, or weird in the best way. And I find that, by pushing our children into these bumper-sticker-friendly, conventional buckets, we create two significant problems that infuse our children with anxiety about their futures. First, we are leaving that which is special about many of our children, those talents and interests quite specific to them, entirely on the table. They are forced into classes and fields in which they have either no acumen or no interest.

I've been there myself, as my bachelor's degree in accounting collects dust. My years in that profession produced enormous anxiety in me that took years to mitigate. It took years away from following interests that were not only fulfilling to me, but a far better use of my gifts, and curiously, more profitable than my accounting career was ever going to be. Clearly, allowing your child to follow her interests and encouraging her to do so is precisely what will bring her success. Form-fitting her into an "acceptable" résumé, on the other hand, will result in anxiety, feelings of failure, dismay, and perhaps hopelessness, as well as a wretched loss of time and talent.

Because of the narrow definition of success we are collectively thrusting upon them, too many of our kids feel discouraged about their lives and their futures. Don't set up the boring, narrow drone path for them. This is lazy parenting and among the worst stories we can write for our children. The culture around us, our schools, our neighborhoods, our extended families, fuel this tired narrative. As parents, we have to guide our children toward their own light, not some false narrative generated to satisfy other people's definition of success.

It is this last point that presents the second major problem, more cultural and societal than personal. When we force conformity in our kids, we are leaving an awful lot of unique talent untapped. I shudder to consider the global implications of this shortsightedness. Not long ago, for instance, I worked with a young man whose parents were deeply concerned with how unusually he presented. Both parents conformed to very linear paths, attending mainstream schools, working jobs expected of business majors. Mom was very social. Dad was a marathoner and financier. They were both happy and successful. For some time, however, they made the mistake of believing that their formula for success would, and should, be their son's formula as well.

But from a young age, he was drawn to different things than they were. He played with Legos for hours. He watched YouTube videos of people dismantling and putting together computers and cell phones. He not only played and enjoyed video games, but examined them like a science, curious as to how the images and game play were initially created. His parents brought him to therapy to socialize and "normalize" him. He was thirteen.

Luckily, these were intelligent parents with open minds. Over time, they came to accept that their son functioned differently than some other kids. His interests were not bumper sticker catchphrases. He was not drawn to convention in any way. So, they stepped back and allowed him space to pursue his interests, passions, and pursuits. It was quite a journey for this family.

Through high school, things just got weirder in this young man's life, in the best way. He developed an interest in 3D printing technology and felt the state of the art in this area was markedly uninventive and unimpressive. He created a vision and worked toward it with impressive vigor. He decided he would build his own printer, one with capacity far beyond anything that currently existed. To make room for his project, he moved his bed into his closet. He filled his room with large tools and tiny electronics. He frequently worked long into the night, fitting homework in where he could.

And he created a product that he believes will revolutionize an industry, perhaps several industries: a 3D printer with very few limitations. He believes his work will impact business, technology, medicine, cars, and more. There is actually huge corporate interest already, and he believes he will make millions, soon. I believe him too. He works like Gates, philosophizes like Jobs, and innovates like Musk. He is happy and thriving himself, and grateful that his parents allowed him to take his life in this unusual direction. When I met him, he never smiled and rarely spoke. Now, he smiles constantly, presents his work with confidence and joy to a wide range of audiences, and is excited for the future.

Again, just a few years ago, he presented as weird and awkward. He didn't fit quite right into the acceptable mold. But I shudder to consider the possibility that his parents would have shut him down through these past few years and forced him into convention. I would have been treating a very anxious, likely depressed, and perhaps hopeless young man. And all that brilliance would never have seen the light of day.

Sometimes, it takes just a moment free of fear, judgment, and ego to allow you the space to make the best, most impactful parenting decisions. You can do this for your child just as readily as these parents did for theirs. And the benefits might be difficult to conceptualize, perhaps impossible to measure, from where you sit today. But if you simply pause and ask yourself if the path you are encouraging is consonant with that child you know, weird or conventional, the best answers will come to you quickly. If you allow yourself to be clouded by your own fears, judgments, and ego, you may increase that anxiety and identity traffic unnecessarily. And the final product may be nothing like the ideal you are hoping for.

Kids are smart, insightful, and keenly intuitive. Your job is to encourage these traits in them. Focus on curating and supporting your child's life force. The right answers will rise to the surface pretty easily if you can be available to do that.

Remember, we are not here to guide kids toward our own images, nor are we here to push them toward convention. We are here, rather, to guide them, to listen, through the fog of all those stimuli, to their own inner voices. We are open to any and all definitions of success. That's mighty parenting.

Roads Less Traveled toward Success

Let's consider some less conventional ways that your child may show she is successful. First, we often forget to celebrate the creativity in our children. This is a missed opportunity. For every child is creative in some way. Your child may be an aspiring rapper, painter, singer, or woodworker. She may sculpt, draw, write, or otherwise express her creativity. Regardless, I strongly urge you to pause here for a moment. We underestimate how art and creative pursuits provide clues, either direct or indirect, into our child's greatest strengths that may lead to a vocation or provide glimpses of hope and joy.

You may find that your child is more mechanically than academically adept, inclined toward working with her hands. She may be drawn to social media in a particularly creative way. She may write Harry Potter fan fiction or show talent in tagging and graffiti art or laying down "beats." I find that when parents tamp down that creative drive, anxiety rises in a child. She is being pressed into the narrow definition of success. When parents give that creativity encouragement and space to build, grow, and often morph into other creative disciplines, anxiety decreases precipitously. Kids then tend to find their way in the world far more readily, their creative voice a resounding note in the symphony that will determine their vocation or the ways in which they may choose to spend their free time.

In any event, I think we all know that creativity is part of an enriched, fulfilled life. And it is often our own parental fears that quash and discourage the creative enterprises of our children. Silence that fear, and trust that her creativity may just lead her to a more fulfilling, happier, well-rounded, and less anxious adulthood.

College Choices and Stressors

I refer to bumper stickers a lot, as I find them quite telling. And I think we all notice that, once our child gains admission to a college, especially an elite school, we are inclined to rush to that bookstore to secure a bumper sticker or license plate frame alerting the world to our pride. And that's pride in our child's accomplishment, to be sure. But it's also pride in ourselves, yes? We have made it to the Parental Promised Land. Not only is our child grown, but she is about to fly with aplomb and greatness and a sense of regal pomp.

We have won parenting. Why wouldn't we celebrate?

That's all fine, in my opinion, provided we honor the path of our child, in lieu of dictating that path, along the way. This distinction is ever-so-tricky to traverse for parents, I find. For, even in this book, I am asking you alternatively to honor your child's path, while recognizing and intervening when she's in trouble, while playing the "parent card" when she's disengaged altogether.

What, exactly, am I asking of you? Fair question.

I am asking you, in any situation including this one, to consider that the best fit for your child is one that will best foster competence, resilience, and *happiness*.

We share this inclination to press our kids toward the highest possible level of achievement through high school. With the very best of intentions, we want our children to move through their lives with ample doors open before them, the world as their oyster. So, AP classes are a good idea, for sure. Loading them up with extracurricular activities: sports, groups, councils, committees, plays, clubs, and volunteer efforts all further the cause. Hours and hours of homework are the only way to push through a rigorous high school curriculum, of course. And then, when the time comes to apply to college, we want the best ones, right? We want our kids to attend one of the Ivies, or, if not, the best-ranked school they can gain admittance into.

Well, if I ever was, I'm no longer supportive of any of that. I find that kids as young as sixth graders are already fully considering, and ruminating over, the college they may attend one day, and feel their preparation needs to start now, lest they fall behind. Most of them, by the way, fear they will. And let's be honest, we are thinking about it that early as well. Does she need to be in a more advanced English class to set her up for APs in high school? Does she need to be involved in travel softball in order to have an opportunity for a scholarship? We press, as we want to keep the doors of opportunity open.

But at what cost?

Pressing our child through middle school and high school into a lifestyle that is out of balance in the service of some future self that can relax because she will have arrived, is, I find, folly. For you are setting a mindset at a young age that is likely to stick with your child for many years, perhaps for a lifetime. A mind does not ease just because of an accomplishment or because some time has passed. No, the better answer is to teach balance. If that means Bs, that means Bs. This is a component of our broadening definition of success. It does not show up solely on a report card. We have to consider the lifestyle that matches our child's personality, along with her strengths and interests.

As one of my heroes, Glennon Doyle, asks frequently, "Is there a better option for our high schoolers than to work themselves sick to get into colleges where they'll work themselves sick to get jobs where they'll work themselves sick?" There has got to be a better way for our kids than this hamster wheel.

It's crucial to note here that success for her may not much resemble what you have been envisioning her entire life. We are looking to foster an individualized definition of success, after all, one that matches her, not your vision for her.

What I'm getting at here is goodness of fit, finding that school that suits her most.

Even if it is not the campus you envisioned. Even if it's not *your* favorite. This is her life and her story. The more you recognize, accept, and embrace your role as a significant but supporting character, the more likely you are to foster a positive and progressive direction for her.

Here's a little comfort. A very recent report in *Time* found evidence that it does not matter, at all, where your child goes to college. It does not matter. The fact that she goes matters, but the name of the school does not. My experience clinically matches this headline but goes further. I find that it does matter a bit. For, if your child opts for a "reach" school, especially upon your urging (or, as in some cases I'm familiar with, your writing a letter to a dean, or sitting on a board, or endowing a school with big money), she may find herself in shock and overstressed once on campus.

Here's how that often goes. A teenager fights through her high school years to achieve in every way she can, leveraging her résumé and maximizing her ACT and SAT scores. Upon graduation, she proudly, exhaustedly, sits very near the top of her class. She heads off to her highly prestigious campus with plans to conquer this larger world in the same way. Upon arriving, however, she realizes that everyone there is an overachieving, Type A, driven academic rock star. Despite all of her achievement, in fact, she may quickly find herself at the bottom of her class for the first time in her life.

This is a highly stressful and disheartening situation in and of itself, to be sure. But it runs deeper than that. Her confidence rapidly begins to wane. Her stress level becomes more noticeable, and sometimes unmanageable. Many college kids I've worked with in this situation have switched majors to something they perceive as more manageable, even if it falls outside their interests. I have worked in situations like this in which the student turns to drugs, often those intended for ADHD or other amphetamines, to keep studying into the night. Or they choose a benzodiazepine, such as Xanax, Ativan, or

Klonopin, to ease their anxious minds. As these are, of course, all highly accessible on every campus in the country, abuse of these drugs becomes a very real possibility, and I have worked with this situation many times in recent years. In the extreme, a lot of these kids drop out of their elite schools, their narrative shattered, broken, and confused. They are often then relegated to community colleges, jobs, and therapy for a time, as they decompress, regroup, and redirect.

This process is, I find, highly predictable from about middle school or so. And it is wholly unnecessary. If you focus on balance and goodness of fit and emotional wellness, your child's path takes on a bright new light. But it takes a degree of courage on the part of parents to let that light shine, as it were. For we need to give up some vision of *our* dreams for our child, in the service of their own, some of which have likely not yet come into focus at all. This requires a dramatic show of faith that your child is capable of discovering her path on her own, if you are willing to take a large enough step back to allow for it.

There is a great deal of joy available to parents if they are willing to allow their child's story to take shape. It requires the most parental availability, as free as reasonable from fear, judgment, and ego. And you can further allow your child to skip some of the painful steps outlined above. Otherwise, you may find yourself pressing your agenda, presumably in the service of your child's best interests. Consider the recent college admissions scandal for just a moment. By way of reminder, some high-profile celebrity parents were caught effectively paying off colleges to gain admission for their children or fraudulently claiming they were athletes in sports they never played, a "back door" into some elite schools. In some cases, it seems, the kids were complicit with their parents. In others, maybe not. And my experience would suggest that we have seen just the beginnings of a far larger story here, implicating far more parents and universities in a plot to fraudulently secure admission.

I am not so fast to judge these parents, by the way. I am fully certain that they felt they were acting in the best interests of their child. They wanted their son or daughter to thrive and succeed and likely intended to facilitate that success by buying their way, one way or another, into the best possible institution. I do not question their intent. I do, however, question whether all of this damning, unnecessary activity really would have served the best interests of their kids, even if they hadn't gotten caught (and I believe many parents have not).

Definitely not.

What I suspect these parents forgot, somewhere in the race for the narrow definition of success, is that their children would not have accomplished anything at all in gaining admission this way. On some level, whether express or implied, these kids would know that their admission was not earned. And their parents would have failed to provide them the opportunity to show themselves both competent and resilient, this payoff representing for them a massive show of no-confidence in their own ability to achieve. And remember, these are our core parenting goals. If our kids do not feel competent and resilient, it doesn't matter what school's name is on that admissions letter. But if they know they've earned that next step, whether it be a university, a community college, or some other career, they will also take with them the sense of competence and resilience that will carry them through every storm, and clear day, of their lives.

It is incumbent upon us to foster greatness in our children, and that may well be in an Ivy League school for yours. But for the vast majority of our kids, it is not. It is in a school that suits them, a school they like, surrounded by people they enjoy, a school that provides an environment not just of learning, but of self-discovery and connection with others. Consider all the *relevant* variables. Then, in the end, allow the school choice to be hers.

The Stressed-Out Freshman

One other crucial note is necessary here. That first year in college, that year when so many kids struggle and nearly a third of them need to reset, needs to be approached differently. We need to let kids know that the college years are not nirvana and they are not expected to mold them into "the best years" of their lives. Instead, these young people need full permission to let us know if they are struggling, lonely, disheartened, or discouraged. Nearly every single college freshman I have ever known, and I have known a lot of them, has experienced all of these at some time during that first year away at school. We need to allow them to talk to us about that openly. If you insist on only good news during that Sunday night phone call, you may be unwittingly exacerbating suffering on the other end of the line.

It causes a lot of dissonance and anxiety when you feel the need to depict something to the outside world, all the time, that does not reflect your internal reality.

And please be aware of this phenomenon when talking with other people's children as well. That freshman year can be so very daunting. Don't force kids into a position where they have to feign excitement to get through a conversation. For their sake, open a more honest dialogue. And give them permission to feel less than perfect. It's an enormous gift that costs nothing.

Their Other Social Media

We all know how difficult it is to keep up with the changing nature and modes of social media. Most of us also know the pinch of hurt when we do not accumulate likes, or when we come upon photos in our feeds of the awesome event we were not invited to. To this extent, we can relate a bit to what our teenagers are going through, and the number social media does on them. But it is important to know the nature of the social media your child is using and how it tends to be used. If you think Instagram is the gold standard kids are using today, read on.

In all likelihood, for example, the Instagram account your child shows you, that she allows you to follow, that is positive and bright and shiny and appropriate, is not the only account she has. Notoriously, you need to know that kids are also likely to use a second account, a Finsta, or Fake Insta. It is here that the social media peril may lie for her. Most kids invite a select grouping of their "friends" to access their Finsta. It is here that they'll post pics of themselves or someone else drinking, smoking, partially nude (yep, happens all the time), or doing something else we may deem inappropriate.

I am consistently surprised that smart, very aware young people are blind to the fact that their Finsta account can bite them in many ways, and believe me, it can. Kids screenshot and share so many pieces of what shows up here or on Snapchat. And sometimes, these shots land in the wrong hands. Kids threaten each other. Schools get involved. I can share horror stories of suspensions and expulsions and broken friendships and shattered trust between child and parent. This is a danger zone for our kids, to be sure. Again, our kids need to be reminded that nothing they put online, as clever as a second hidden account may seem, is either temporary or private.

Keep in mind that the list of social media sites here is not even remotely exhaustive and different regions and neighborhoods may use different sites. It is important, for the sake of safety and self-esteem, that you are in on your child's social media world, without being invasive. This is not necessarily the easiest needle you will thread as a parent, but it is an important one.

And social media sites are becoming more and more clever at the art of eluding parents, whether this is intentional on the part of the designers or not. Snapchat, with its disappearing content, is frustrating enough for many parents trying to get a solid bead on their child's life online. But your child may be using a number of other social media sites and privacy tools to elude you. Some photo storage apps, such as Vaulty, for example, offer two password options, one presumably for less private information that a child is likely to offer parents who insist on access. The other allows deeper access to a well of other, typically more intimate, data. Another group of apps, such as Calculator%, hide private data behind an icon that looks wholly innocuous, an awful lot like the iPhone calendar app.

Pretty dastardly and clever, no?

Of course, the sense of security many teens feel, sharing online only with a select group of friends, is often proven to be entirely false. Recently, the *New York Times* published a piece about ten Harvard admits. Each of their admissions had been rescinded for various reasons, but all due to information the Admissions Department was able to identify online. A screenshot, or a minor hacker, can short-circuit a career before it even begins.

The horror stories do not end there. I have worked with a girl whose reputation was quickly ruined because of a photo of a friend, partially dressed, that was screenshotted and subsequently sent to approximately ten thousand other teens in the area. She was intending to capture a private, playful moment getting ready for a dance. Long story short, she was teased and bullied to the extent that she had to switch schools. Further, her father was arrested on child pornography charges. The cell phone containing the initial image was registered under his name.

I also worked with an eighth-grade boy who befriended another boy his age on Snapchat. They planned to meet at this other boy's house. His father discovered their exchange, and the other boy turned out to be not only a full-grown man, but a registered child sex offender. These online mistakes can have legs. As you know by now, I do not think teens have many limitations. But, as their brains are developing, they may be guided so much by the rush of accumulating likes that it short-circuits the more reasoning parts of the mind. So, as much disdain as I hold for the lecture and for snooping, social media can be a matter of health and safety at times. We need to talk with our children, frequently, about safe online behavior. And, if need be, we need to insist on access to passwords for yourself, cousins, aunts, uncles, and anyone else who might be able to help keep your child safe in the wild west of online space.

Also, you need to recognize that you may have a lot to learn about navigating that space. A recent study suggested that the vast majority of teens believe that their parents knew very little, if anything, about their online lives. Follow-up research suggested that these teenagers were mostly correct. I strongly encourage you to shift your thinking around this subject. Most parents I know feel a need to "police" online behavior through TeenSafe or other similar apps. This creates a fear of getting caught by teenagers, who are more capable at navigating the online universe than we are by a significant margin. Further, it creates a divide in your relationship, a cat-and-mouse game, that you can't win.

Instead, come up with a collaborative alliance around online safety, an ongoing discussion about both the risks and rewards of social media. Ask to see her profiles. Ask about the culture online. Ask her to show you how Snapchat works. If you are like most parents, you probably have no idea. Kids are great teachers, and you will learn far more and feel more prepared using this approach. And you will gain the leverage to talk with your kids about some of the stories highlighted above, which may dispel some of the myths they believe about their own online safety.

Given that our teenagers will always likely be several steps ahead of us with regard to social media, the more we guide them toward the development of their own online ethic, the smarter, safer, and better informed they will be.

Now, when we were growing up, many of us engaged in fantasies about what we might do for a living. You may have wanted to be a rock star, a firefighter, a model, an actor. Though most of us took our fantasies and wishes quite seriously, some of this dreaming takes on a different, sometimes urgent tenor for kids today. On Instagram, for instance, kids follow people with millions of followers, "influencers" who monetize their feeds by simply mentioning products.

In short, your kids are aware of the Kardashians and other major influencers, the millions of followers they've attained, and the millions of dollars that have resulted. There are tens of thousands of other people doing the same, some of whom your kids are likely following. They have a feel for how this end of the economy works, far more than most of us do. It's a big part of their lives. And these "influencers" become the litmus test and the metric for far too many of our kids: impossibly beautiful, impossible bodies, impossibly wealthy, with a nearly impossible number of followers. Instagram alone provides the fragile teenager's ego with ample evidence that they are "not good enough." In fact, by the Kardashian metric, they are not even in the league. For our kids using followers and likes as reference points, the Kardashian metric is a dangerous proposition to self-worth.

I have worked with many teenagers who intend to make their millions, not by becoming great athletes or curing cancer, but by becoming Insta-famous. For lack of a clinical impression, I can safely say that, in my experience, this potentiality really messes with kids' heads. Many kids hyperfocus on their feeds and on methods for gaining followers. And we all know that, although many things are possible, the likelihood that your child will be among those that can earn a living off their Instagram posts is slim.

That said, I strongly urge you to handle this parenting issue with a great deal of care. Woven within that wish for Insta-fame is an undertone of ambition, perhaps a penchant for marketing or sales. Be realistic, but please do not be discouraging to your child. You might try to reframe their perception of their feed as an experiment and encourage all the positives that arise from the process. In my experience, not only is there no need to shut it down, but it would be ineffective anyway. Your child will find her way onto social media, and, for her, it is an important method of social connection.

The fallacy that so many of us parents operate within, that can be so damaging to our relationships with our children and their generation, is that, because of this "Kardashian effect," we are raising a generation of vapid, self-centered, egocentric, and amoral people with no concern for the greater good. They want everything for nothing, I've heard, and are just looking to build their own personal "brand," whatever that means.

Well, as it turns out, it can be very meaningful.

As I have described elsewhere here, you do not have to talk with a teenager for very long to recognize that this perception could not be further from the truth. The wishes for wealth and Insta-fame, you quickly find, are not incongruent with a global awareness and a sense of social justice. Both thoughts and wishes can exist in the same mind without clashing and often do. And sometimes, they become one and the same. A friend of mine has a daughter in her early twenties. She has amassed substantial Insta-fame, but her "Insta-mission," if you will, is to protect and preserve the environment. She is well aware that she and her boyfriend are attractive and appealing. So she leverages those qualities into a platform for environmental causes, each post bearing an element of "cuteness," along with a message about conservation, or pollution, or cleaning the oceans.

Pretty brilliant use of a brand and platform, wouldn't you say?

In fact, your children are so aware of what is going on in the world immediately surrounding them, and the world at large, that they are wholly overwhelmed by it all. Due to a deep sense of morality and empathy developed too early on, they are unsure what useful, impactful role, if any, they can possibly play. I am heartened by the fact that so many kids want their positive voices heard through their presence on social media, promoting social justice or a certain brand of politics or eliminating the stigma of mental illness. Once they realize they have a voice, something important to say, they feel quite empowered by the fact that they have a ready-made platform from which to say it. And sometimes, lacking solutions to offer one another, they offer encouragement and a sense that nobody is suffering alone. I suspect immeasurable suffering has been diluted, diminished, or eliminated altogether as a result. I am also virtually certain that many young lives have been saved through encouragement on social media. Seriously.

Part Two

ADDRESSING THE ISSUES

Anxiety

Your teenager is anxious. I know this for a fact. She may not have a diagnosis of panic disorder or OCD. But she is anxious. She is fearful. Most teenagers are well aware of these feelings in themselves. Some are not.

Recently, I spoke with a crowd of parents after a showing of *Angst*, a documentary about teenage anxiety. Several parents were perplexed, suggesting that their kids have everything they need, so what exactly are they anxious about? Well, it's a very good question, and a fair one. But the answer is quite complicated.

For I find that kids are existentially anxious about a lot. They are anxious about the meaning of life, specifically the meaning of their own lives. They are anxious about money, and whether they will have it. They are anxious about terrorism, social welfare, the rise of student debt, climate change, and the state of political discourse. They are anxious about everything we are anxious about, and more. They are anxious when school portals are updated or when they fail to be. They are anxious when they feel the mini seismic jolt of a notification on their phone, buzzing in their pocket. They are anxious when alerts of another school shooting pop up on their phone while they are sitting in a school.

At a different showing of *Angst*, I conducted a Q&A session with the audience. The first to raise his hand with a question was a young boy who told me about how anxious he is about school, his social life, concern about college, and how to build a happy, less anxious life for himself. He was nine years old. So yes, even our very young kids carry a sense of looming anxiety and an awareness of the passage of time and the scope of their lives that their young minds have a great deal of difficulty understanding without a great deal of undue anxiety.

These are anxious times, and the degree of anxiety I hear about from teenagers, younger kids, and young adults is absolutely unprecedented and growing exponentially. I work with Lisa, for instance, a girl who is at the very top of her high school class of around a thousand. She is a skilled academic, musician, and athlete. But she is scared. She fears the house of cards will fall. She fears she is not well-liked. She is virtually certain she is unlovable, so she fears she will be alone, not just through her teen years, but for a lifetime. Most of us didn't think like Lisa when we were her age. Conveniently, we lacked the scope of "a lifetime." We were cushioned from such grand considerations by a trickle of information entering our young minds, not a waterfall. Kids today are far more aware. There are a lot of Lisas out there.

But on the other end of the bell curve lies the lazy, basement-dwelling, homework-avoidant, screen-addicted, vape-addled crowd. This "lowest quarter," as one of my Type A clients lovingly calls them, make up for the rest for the lack of anxiety they must be suffering, right?

Nope. Believe it or not, I have learned that this group is just as anxious as their overachieving colleagues, if not more so. They have chosen a different path, opting out of virtually all elements of that hyper-competitive life. They are underperforming, to be sure. Yet that choice likely comes from a recognition that they do not want that moment-to-moment, day-to-day stress in their lives. So, this group is in hiding. But the underperforming itself is stressful. Added to that is the anxiety of not knowing where you might be headed from here. As a result, this group does tend to self-medicate with something, be it drugs, alcohol, video games, binge-watching, or some other distraction or diversion, all of them anxiety-provoking in their own right.

All of that is to say, few children today escape anxiety. Unwittingly, we have left them with an anxiety-inducing set of cultural circumstances. Most of us are keenly aware of the physical and emotional sensations that set the hallmarks of anxiety. If you are lucky enough to suffer it very little, let me describe it to you, for I have suffered from anxiety and panic issues throughout my life and have treated them hundreds of times.

Short of chronic pain, I'm not sure there is a more uncomfortable physical sensation than anxiety. Sufferers describe almost any physical symptom you can think of, from dizziness to nausea to headaches to joint pain. Anxiety is a most clever psychological predator, isolating and highlighting the symptoms we most fear. Some people, like myself, have experienced the sharp, undeniable, acute symptoms of a panic attack, a wretched half hour or so of excruciating fear that arrives seemingly out of thin air. Most of us experience a more chronic, ongoing state of anxiety, a persistent buzz of fear in the back of the brain, permeating one's days and nights. Anxiety is a grand disruptor of our normal functioning. It can run our thoughts and virtually our entire lives, even when we are not fully aware we are suffering from it.

And anxiety feeds on itself. We become anxious about being anxious.

Anxiety takes many forms, and tracking anxiety in kids is like a feckless game of Whack-a-Mole. Some experience overt, acute panic attacks. Some feel uncomfortable enough in school that they refuse to go. Some panic during tests or public speaking. Some experience acid reflux or other physical symptoms that are deeply rooted in their anxiety. Some experience the hyperkinetic impulse to vape, or grab their phone, or act out, all a manifestation of profound anxiety.

"Am I doing enough?"

"Am I good enough?"

"Do I have a chance?"

"Do I even have what it takes to make it?"

"Can I sustain a life for myself and my family the way my parents have?"

I see these kids, and they are strong, kind, fun, funny, loving, caring young people. I see kids who want to make a difference in the world and are afraid they may not find their way. I see kids who have the courage to ask the big questions—Why am I here? What is my purpose? Why am I engrossed in minutiae when there are so many other people with so many more pressing difficulties? I see better people, kinder, deeper, more thoughtful people, with each passing year. These kids make me happy. They make me laugh. And every day, they leave me with enormous hope for the future—even if they themselves are suffering the depths of depression and anxiety.

The problem: this is not what they see in themselves. What they see is too often ugly, or weird, or unlovable, unworthy of a simple invite or like. I find that kids fear, not only that they are unimportant, but that they are wholly *unnecessary*. Consider this thought for a moment. Imagine feeling quite certain, at a very young age, that your very existence is unimportant, unnecessary, and inconvenient. Many kids are not only afraid that they are not fundamentally good, but that they may be flat-out toxic to others. Not only will you fail to make a positive impact on the world, but you are fundamentally a detriment to those around you.

The pluck and strength of the Parkland high school students taking a microphone within days of bearing witness to the mass shooting of their friends, in their school—that's the spirit I see in this entire generation. Those kids were unwittingly given a reason to move, to shake off the anxious fog and act. Their courage rose quickly to the surface in the wake of shock, when a typical inclination might well be to hole up and isolate, to self-protect. The good we see in those young people is out there among virtually all of them. We just need solutions short of a massive crisis to elicit that strength from them.

Blessedly, most of our kids have not experienced this type of marked, life-altering trauma. But I believe that, just below the surface of anxiety and self-loathing borne by so many children, that type of courage and strength and kindness exists. I want to help you find ways for your child to see these qualities in herself without a crisis precipitating her awareness. That's our tricky mandate here.

Short of crisis, I find solutions come in smaller bites when it comes to anxiety. Regardless of where they fall on the bell curve of action, our anxious kids require the experience of some wins. Wins are more easily conceptualized for the underperformers. For this group, wins can come in small steps. For those suffering profound anxiety who refuse to go to school, for instance, a week managing that anxiety in the classroom counts as a win. For the C student, a B on a test counts, for sure. Regardless, it's also important that we meet our kids where they are and appreciate the strengths they currently have, even if they are not measured on an attendance sheet or a report card. So, if your child is an aspiring rapper (as many kids are today), give their music a listen and provide them some feedback. If they are Insta-fabulous (as one of my clients has deemed herself), check out her social media feeds. You might be surprised there. Be open to that. You may have a budding dancer on your hands—I've worked with a lot of kids with killer moves. Your child's strengths may not be what you would have chosen, but they come by them honestly. We are missing a mighty parenting opportunity, and driving depression and anxiety, if we dismiss these passions and strengths as folly, worthless, or unacceptable. There's a chance to relieve anxiety here and build self-worth.

Now, I fully recognize that I am asking you to relinquish a lot here. But to be clear, I am not suggesting you forgo all parenting and allow your child to do nothing. Nor am I suggesting that underperforming is okay. But if you find yourself lecturing and punishing and pressing and micromanaging, if you are working harder for her success than she is, then you need a different solution, a fresh starting point. I find that, once esteem is built—through acceptance, grades, chores—other behaviors tend to buoy up rather naturally. But without that recognition of where your child is in her life currently, she feels as if she is floating aimlessly and alone, and further, she is fully aware of your contempt. It drains the Emotional Bank Account, and self-worth lands at a standstill. Anxiety rises, probably for both of you. This is the set of circumstances that is filling up therapists' schedules across the nation.

For kids on the other end of the spectrum, the overachievers, wins come in a very different package, and parenting here is every bit as tricky. The fairly natural inclination would be to praise and support their behavior, as it fits perfectly into our narrow definition of success and doesn't look too shabby on our parental report card either. None of us is, frankly, ashamed of our Honor Roll student, right? But relinquishing that need to be perfect is the actual win here. You need to know that your perfect child likely focuses on her imperfections far too often. Perfectionism promotes unrealistic standards in our kids that are often impossible or, at the very least, prohibitive to meet. Again, anxiety rises.

Failing these markers, many kids find themselves opting out, landing in a very different cohort described below. Because they are not resilient to the idea of accepting failure and disappointment as a part of their lives, they are highly susceptible to significant, and sometimes debilitating, anxiety and depression. This perfectionism is, by definition, unrealistic. But some overachievers find disappointment in some strange spaces in their mind. I have worked with many perfectionistic teenagers and college students, for example, who are down on themselves for failing to know some subject matter in school to which they have never even been exposed. This distorted thinking can further exacerbate the related emotional difficulties by a significant margin. Also, these young people are at risk because they are reluctant to seek out help for any emotional difficulties they may be suffering, feeling as if they should be able to manage any issues they suffer on their own. This can be, suffice it to say, a dangerous situation.

My advice for these kids is to let go of those perfectionistic standards a bit, allow yourself to have more fun, and actually protect time for it. Whereas many kids have far too much time on their hands, this Type A group has precious little down time by design. I find that they are often uncomfortable sitting alone with their thoughts, and the prescription is often meditative rather than active. I press these kids to tend better to their emotional well-being the way they do their grades, or their performance in the sports, clubs, plays, ensembles, and other extracurricular groups they belong to.

This focus on emotional well-being is no small thing for this group. The dearth of self-care here is epidemic, and the chronic push for achievement toward perfection is terribly unhealthy. For this reason, I would honestly propose that middle schools and high schools mandate a class on emotional wellness nationwide. First, kids are voracious students for this type of material; so many children whose strengths are not highlighted in other academic areas would thrive here. Also, emotional wellness comprises a critical component of success that we fail to measure or account for in the day-to-day lives of our children. We can all think of many young people who successfully complete a fine résumé, but are chronically unhappy and stressed, for instance.

I worked recently with Dan, a twenty-three-year-old man who excelled to such an extent in his business school that he landed a Wall-Street-level job paying well into the six figures. He bought a sleek car and a very cool condo just a couple blocks from Wrigley Field here in Chicago, home of his favorite team, the Cubs (2016 World Series champions, for those keeping score, and Dan was).

By the time he came to me, he was working seven days a week, eleven- or twelve-hour days. He was pulling in big money, and the future looked super bright for him. But he was wildly anxious, exhausted, and completely out of sync. He pointed out that he had lived in his condo for two years, but he hadn't once set foot in Wrigley, even during the World Series season, much to his dismay. Not that he couldn't afford it—he absolutely could. It was his imbalanced, nearly impossible work schedule that did not allow for it, not once in two years.

As he described it, he worked in a bullpen full of Type A "studs," about thirty young men all looking to strike it rich. Most evenings, by around seven, as the crew began to tire, someone would pull out their prescription for Adderall or Ritalin, and everyone would snort a pill or two to keep sharp into the evening. When I met him, he was heavily addicted to the drug, and it took months to reset his drug-free bearings. But first, he quit the job, recognizing how untenable it was and that it would ruin his emotional well-being, and soon. I'm grateful he had the presence of mind to seek out therapy before that happened. He took a few months, literally went fishing, and caught a few

Cubs games. He then found a nine-to-five that suited him well, just competitive enough to match his drive and ambition, but balanced enough that he felt well emotionally.

His story, of course, could easily have ended differently. I lament the fact that there were twenty-nine other young people in that room, still pressing for the elusive win, addicted to the work and the drug. I'm not sure the story ends so happily for all of them. And that is precisely why balance, and goodness of fit, are more important than prestige for our overachieving young people. We need to collectively get on message here before it's literally too late for some of them.

As you may be recognizing, anxiety in young people is a personal matter for me. Not only have I sat across from far too many young people suffering from it, but I was one of those people. I know the weight of that burden, and how prohibitive it is to bear it for any length of time. Choosing the wrong major, that looked damn good on paper, and taking a job with the wrong firm, that also seemed perfect, I set myself up for chronic anxiety. Daily, I would sneak into a bathroom stall, suffering panic attacks so profound I held onto opposing walls in order to steady myself before returning to work. Only when I sought therapy myself, and quit that job, did I find relief. Anxiety is a helpful messenger in this regard. It's an undeniable clarion call from body to mind suggesting this is an untenable way of life.

I can say with unusual authority that you need to promote this message of balance and goodness of fit to your child.

I personally believe that, if we can collectively deliver that message, that balance and goodness of fit and emotional wellness are the cornerstones of success, we will be helping our kids all across the bell curve. Of course, our overachievers will recognize that they can relax their standards away from perfection for the sake of their well-being, an enormous win in itself. But those who struggle will likely press further, especially with some solid education into the nature of emotional wellness. Specifically, they will learn that they do not need to check out in order to spare themselves. Remember, checking out is itself anxiety-inducing.

Otherwise, we will continue to widen this growing chasm between, on one hand, young people fighting to get into the most prestigious schools only to feel, at some point in the future, exhausted, anxious, disheartened, and unsatisfied with the narrative of their lives, and on the other, more and more kids opting out, refusing to go to school or underperforming when they do, undervaluing their strengths, and smoking pot, vaping, drinking, or turning to other drugs to manage their anxiety.

The burden of this would not just be borne on an individual basis, by the way. We are already overtaxing our kids and leaving an awful lot of talent untapped, either due to opting out or burning out. And we need these good, thoughtful, empathic, and talented children and future leaders, now more than ever. These are trying times, politically, culturally, and otherwise, and this next generation has, I can assure you, all the talent and energy needed to right our collective ship. But we need to do our part as a generation in setting the stage for them. I stand by the idea that a course in emotional well-being would be an enormous step forward in getting there. In the meantime, we need to provide the emotional space for wellness in our homes. It is on us, the parents, to do so. This is our mandate.

And this, to me, is among the best stuff of life, truly. To sit with a fifteen-year-old, who is so deep and thoughtful and brilliant, but suffering, and to have the privilege of hearing her out, is amazing. Knowing that, just in deeply listening, we are helping alleviate that anxiety—what a precious gift we parents possess. Just bearing witness, and really seeing and hearing your brilliant child, is, to my thinking, why we are here. This is among the greatest joys of my life, to be sure.

Heightened Awareness

Kids today are exposed to material that we were able to protect children from only a few short years ago. I frequently tell the story of how my wife and I managed the flow of information in the immediate aftermath of the terror of 9/11, when my son was not yet six years old. First, in the pre-iPad age, we simply turned off the TV when George was in the room. We didn't discuss the matter with him and went about our day as normally as possible so that his tender mind could not discern any apparent difference in our affect.

We controlled the narrative that day, because we could.

On September 12, 2001, I took George out to our backyard and we lay on our backs looking up. As we lived on a flight path leading into and out of the typically bustling O'Hare airport outside Chicago, I asked him to look up and let me know what felt different. After a few guesses, he recognized there were no airplanes in the sky that day. It was quiet. He remembers that, and, as he developed and we felt he could manage to comprehend and integrate the nature of the trauma, we slowly told him more and more about the day and the ensuing challenges on the world stage.

Were such an incident to take place tomorrow, God forbid, parents would have no agency over the narrative. Through an iPad, TV, other screen, or other child, your eight-year-old would know, within moments, that something tragic had taken place. Your *five-year-old* would know.

And these children would have no way of comprehending and assimilating the reality of a moment like that. Developmentally, their brains are not there yet. But we no longer have the luxury of time. Because of that early flow of data, kids are finding out about events they cannot comprehend, pragmatically or emotionally. When people are awful in their behavior online, with hate speech and vitriol, our kids know, right away. They are overwhelmed with the constant volume and flow of information from the earliest years of their lives. It strikes me how many children are entirely unfamiliar with silence.

The fallout of this phenomenon is nearly impossible to calculate. Many kids do not know what it feels like to have a quiet mind for even a moment. The space between each thought for them is filled with bytes of information accumulated from screens and earbuds and other surrounding stimuli. Upon a moment's consideration, this is rather alarming. Most of us can recall a time when our mind was not anxious. We can think back to a moment that was, quite literally, carefree. I'm not sure that is true of kids today. They carry burdens, heavy on their brows. They worry and pick and move on to the next thing without pausing to consider. Or they peer into the same black mirror hour after hour, anxious energy accumulating in their bodies and minds. It's a brutal reality to think about, but one we need to face.

The antidotes for all the noise are contrary to each other, oddly. First, we need to ensure our kids are occupied, and moving, and playing, that their eyes are up for the vast majority of their waking hours. Start this young and it will be easier to maintain, just as a body in motion tends to stay in motion.

But we also need to promote the idea of stillness in our kids, of the importance and art of a quiet and meditative body and mind. This, again, is where a course in emotional well-being would be a brilliant new educational pillar. In the meantime, of course, we need to create space for a quiet mind, at peace, at home.

My son was a high school swimmer. His coach, Scott Walker, a brilliant, caring man who was no soft touch, was a guest on our podcast recently. He pointed out that, early in the morning before school and after school for a couple of hours, the guys on that team found sanctuary in that natatorium. Imagine the peace of being in the water, focused on the swim, for hours a day. That is the type of situation that allows for a quiet and meditative mind, a mind that has enough remaining bandwidth to absorb the onslaught of stimuli the rest of the day will offer, knowing that the sanctuary of the pool would be there for them the next day, and the day after that, and so on. I can say with authority that George benefited greatly from having this sanctuary. It provided a sense of balance, and ease of emotional self-regulation, a most important skill these days. Years later, he retains that capacity. And when he meets a tipping point for the toxic combination of stimuli and anxiety, he utilizes what has become a natural inclination toward exercise, zeroing in on his own self-made sanctuary.

This is fast becoming one of the most important skills we can master.

Now, I realize that not every child will be a swimmer. But there are many ways to provide that type of physical and emotional sanctuary. Practice for most other sports allows for it. Playing music in a band, choir, or orchestra allows for it. If you think about it, essentially any activity that is absorbing and creates a natural distance between a teen and a screen allows for it. So, think about your home for a moment, and how life plays out for your child at home. Is there space for sanctuary, for the healing of the mind, body, and spirit? If not, I strongly urge you to consider ways to provide that. This may comprise a family bedtime ritual, for instance. I work with one family that puts down all screens around nine thirty, for instance, and talks or plays a game before bed. That's some pretty good sanctuary. A father I work with is teaching his entire family the Transcendental Meditation exercises that have brought him profound peace of mind.

Sanctuary.

Where can it be found for your child, in your home?

There is another benefit worth noting to that sanctuary and the play and movement of the mind and body. Your child will realize, in the pool, on the stage, or the court or field, that she owns agency over something amazing and important in her life. And there is so much power in that agency, in knowing you have control in an important space in your life. It suggests control elsewhere. And that is an antidote to anxiety.

Healthy Revisions

Sometimes, I find, we become blind to the activity in our homes that is unhealthy, especially in light of this heightened awareness that precludes the availability of sanctuary. I often suggest that my client families take an inventory of daily activities that are crying out for revision in this regard, begging for something more productive and healthy. I have run into answers as varied as the following:

- Turn off the television that is perpetually on and creating unnecessary auditory and visual noise, and driving up anxiety for the entire family

- Screen-free meals (not nearly as common as you may think)

- Collect phones from your kids and friends and place them in a bowl by the front door. Kids tend to engage with one another *far* more without them, of course

- Talking more slowly, deliberately, and quietly to one another in your home

- Playing calming music throughout the house

All of these ideas, and many you may have yourself, are all intended to balance the heightened awareness all of our kids (and we ourselves) carry, for better or worse. Families have told me that many of these revisions have improved home life enormously for them. You will find more ideas below in the section titled "The Vibe in Your Home."

Awareness of Mental Illness

When you were a teenager, how many of your friends were depressed? How many were anxious? How about bipolar? How many suffered ADHD? Was anyone you knew suicidal?

Some of you may have pretty concise answers to these questions, but I'll bet most of you do not. I know I don't. Truth is, barring some significant, truly profound difficulties, mental illness and emotional diagnoses were not discussed when we were kids. Perhaps they were stigmatized, creating some unnecessary additional suffering. That is certainly not the case today. Today, kids are keenly aware, not just of the notion of mental and emotional suffering, but of all of the above diagnoses and more. Many kids receive one or more mental illness diagnoses before they cross the threshold into high school.

Along with the idea of mental illness comes the idea of potentially needing tools for *coping* with one's suffering. Consider your own childhood. In all likelihood, the idea of coping tools or mechanisms was outside your vernacular until much later in life. Barring some profound, obvious difficulties, most of us just, well, coped. We may not have felt mighty, but we were far less aware of the idea that we might not be able to cope with our day-to-day lives.

But today, just as mental illness is a part of the discussion, coping is a part of it as well. And kids cope in many, many different ways. Some avail themselves of useful tools, where others utilize wildly maladaptive methods for coping. Many of

the kids I see, for example, ask their parents to let them see a
therapist as they sense they need to work something through
verbally with someone objective, not Mom or Dad. If your child
ever asks to talk with someone, by the way, I strongly urge you
to heed the message. Kids do not request therapy frivolously.
They always have a reason, and I cannot think of a more
adaptive, healthy, lifelong tool for coping with virtually any
difficulty than the power of talk therapy.

But we all know that kids today often choose, and have readily
available to them, myriad methods of maladaptive coping.
There are drugs available to them, both prescription and
recreational. The difference is not always as clear as you may
think, by the way. What may start out as a script for Adderall
or Xanax for symptom management, a certain kind of coping,
can devolve into "over-coping" through abuse of the very drugs
prescribed to help. The dangers rise with certain drugs, as we
know. Most of us have been touched in some way by the opioid
crisis sweeping across the nation. Person by person, almost any
addiction, even the most lethal, can often be traced back to an
innocent wish to cope with some difficulty.

Of course, kids don't always cope through drugs. Video games,
social media, food, and even an evening of "Netflix and chill"
can all be seen as coping mechanisms, and reasonably harmless
in moderate doses. But we also know that any of these can
be addictive in their own ways, coping run amuck, creating
problems of excess that seem at first to be behavioral in nature,
but upon a moment's analysis, are driven by a perceived
need to cope.

Nowhere do I find evidence that Generation Z is enfeebled more than in the strikingly common diagnosis these days of "school refusal," an apparent phobic reaction to school attendance. Consider this scenario: when a child is told, by her therapist or physician, that she suffers school refusal, the suggestion right in the diagnostic title is the idea that she cannot manage and cope with the school day, and that somehow what most other children can appear to breeze through with ease is prohibitive for her. It is perhaps the most disempowering diagnosis I deal with regularly. More than once, I have asked a new client why he or she has missed so many days of school in the past semester.

"I can't go. I have school refusal."

Can you read here how just the language alone suggests weakness, an absolute inability to cope? We need to attend better to the language we use, utilize far more strength-based phrases to describe our children, and recognize when we are disempowering them. Labeling them with a psychiatric diagnosis ("She's depressed." "She's bipolar." "She's an anorexic." "She has school refusal.") can be somewhat disempowering, for instance.

Now, there is a clear counterpoint here as well. Some children are so anxious they have difficulty making it to school. Some children do suffer from eating disorders and anxiety, attention difficulties or depression. And I have found that knowing their difficulty has a name, and that other people suffer from it as well, can actually be quite a relief and quite empowering. I am stressing here that we want to be sensitive to the labels we apply to our children, as they are likely to take ownership of them.

If your child suffers a mental health issue, talk them through the label. Help them to seek out the help they need. But be sure to temper it with a belief, from you, that they are capable and competent. That they have strengths that will carry them through. Otherwise, the label becomes core to their sense of identity, and I find this to be disempowering and unhealthy.

Let's think about school refusal again for a moment. Believe me, it does a child no favors to keep them out of school for a prolonged period of time because they are anxious about the day. The longer they are allowed to stay away, the more difficult it is to get them, behaviorally, to return. But worse, the cancer of self-doubt sets hard over a very short period of time. And, too often, a diagnosis like this—more the description of an anxiety symptom than a diagnosis—creates a *patient* out of a child, and leaves her vigilant for the physical or emotional responses that suggest she cannot cope.

Consider this for just a moment, and you will easily recognize that this is not at all what you want for your child and not at all what she needs. In fact, she needs just the opposite, language that shows her how strong, and intelligent, and competent, and resilient she is. She needs to know that you know that she can manage any setback. And if she suffers a difficulty on any given day, she needs to know that you are there for her, that you have her back in every way.

That is empowering.

Another area in which I find we tend to disempower our children lies in the unclear diagnostic space of test anxiety. Like other areas of performance anxiety, including public speaking, sports, and social situations, test anxiety is, to a degree, expected. If you stop and consider the nature of an exam for a moment, there are a number of skills being evaluated. First and foremost, of course, educators are looking to ensure children have mastered the material they are being taught. Tests are typically time-limited, so we are also measuring the degree to which they can effectively manage time. For most subjects, students also need to develop a strategy for taking a test effectively. They may do the easiest questions first, read through the test before beginning, or circle areas they're struggling with to return to them later in the session.

But woven in there also, whether it is deliberate or not, lies a child's ability to manage their own anxiety in real time. Throughout their education, and, into their work life, this will prove to be an invaluable skill. It is also, I find, a skill that most children possess. But sometimes, coming from a place of empathy, I believe, we parents can disempower our children in this regard. If they come to us suggesting that they choked on a particular exam, for instance, we may be quick to label this test anxiety, as disempowering a label as school refusal, to my thinking.

The unspoken suggestion here is that all anxiety is negative, maladaptive, and needs to be managed and avoided. But the truth is, without a moderate, manageable degree of stress and anxiety, we would underperform just as readily as we would when overly anxious. The goal, therefore, is to find the right balance, a middle ground where stress is managed well and performance is maximized. But in order to get there, we need to teach our kids that they are resilient and that they can manage a moderate degree of stress and anxiety. In fact, for nearly every day for the rest of their lives, they will need to do precisely that. If we don't prepare them for this, if we provide them the message that they are only going to manage when free of anxiety, we are setting them up for heartbreak and, ultimately, failure. This is among the most important lessons we can teach our children—that they are resilient, that we know they are resilient, and that we are confident that they can manage all that is expected of them in this world. Just imagine the skyrocketing degree of anxiety that would ensue if we teach them anything to the contrary.

We need to bolster the reality that our kids are capable in school, socially, in their sport, and otherwise. This is one of the most important goals of parenting.

Too often, as parents, we respond in a hair-trigger fashion to behaviors we find maladaptive or counterproductive. This reaction is nearly always a misfire, and the underlying misunderstanding can lead to years of frustration, disconnection, and pain in both parent and child. I really want you to know that the lion's share of that suffering can be avoided. But, in order to do so, it is critical that you take a moment, and consider the emotional underpinnings of the behavior you find maladaptive: the drug or alcohol use, the "laziness," the poor grades, the wrong crowd, the bad attitude.

What suffering is being coped with here?

Remember, nobody *wants* to be the kid who isn't thriving. Your child may claim this is what she wants, and that she just wants to be left alone. But you need to recognize the reality, to lead the way for her, dig deep in order to give her permission to do the same. Believe me, when you lift the veil and get to the emotional realities, everything improves very quickly. Behavior and attitudes and grades can bounce back easily, even gracefully. Your connection will not only return, but deepen. You will have visited a deeper, more emotional space together. And once you do that, you can hold that shared safe space to revisit whenever you need it. Most of life, of course, will take place a little closer to the surface. That's human nature, and not much gets accomplished, homework or practice or developing relationships, if you sit in that space forever.

But it needs to be there for the two of you to visit together when needed. This is the safe emotional space you create when you tend to the Emotional Bank Account with your child. It is why the EBA is so crucial, not only to your relationship, but also to your child's well-being.

The availability of that space will prove priceless to your child and will provide you with great relief and a tool for reconnecting. This "safe space" tool can mitigate so much unnecessary coping for your child as well and may help them avoid some of the "over-coping" pitfalls.

I am well aware that this advice runs directly counter to what you often hear reflects good parenting these days, as well as the tools available to us as parents. We have portals and tracking apps and parental controls and nanny cams. We have the email addresses for teachers and deans, counselors, advisors, and principals. Much of what is available for parents suggests that good parents engage in nearly constant behavior analysis.

Why wouldn't we use an app that tracks specifically how much time our child spends on each of their social media apps every day? Why wouldn't we write the math teacher if our daughter is not reporting her grades frequently enough?

Addressing these questions with parents is virtually a daily occurrence in my office. And my advice for parents is, unless your child provides you with specific cause for concern, skip the apps and the portals and the tracking almost altogether. They are a collective trap, drawing you into a situation in which you are, in effect, spying on your child every day as a matter of habit. It's unhealthy and fundamentally disempowering. These "tools" take up an undue amount of your time and energy, while drawing down the trust built up between you and your child. They are a broad show of no-confidence in your child and do nothing to further either competence or resilience.

One other disturbing yet significant phenomenon is noteworthy here. From YouTube to every form of social media to secret online groups specifically designed for the mentally ill teenager, the Internet plays a potent role in many aspects of the teenager's awareness of mental illness and the fragility of their own well-being. A quick Google search will provide any teen with support, and the message that she is not alone with her suffering. On the other hand, a slightly different search will provide far darker, more subversive information. Teens can find tutorials on methods for self-harm that will go undetected by parents, for instance. They can easily locate information on effective methods for non-lethal suicidal gestures, as well as surefire means of suicide completion. I have done some research here and found alarming sites that effectively encourage depression, dark and suicidal thinking and gestures, and profound anxiety in teenagers.

Parents can handle this phenomenon in a couple of different ways. We all know we can purchase pricey blocks and filters that prevent access to certain sites or allow access to only a select few. We can turn off the Wi-Fi whenever our kids do not need it for homework. We can keep devices in public areas of our homes. I have no problem with any of these interventions.

But I don't want any parent reading this to lull themselves into a false sense of comfort here. Restricting access in the confines of your home does not restrict access everywhere, for instance. Any other device may well allow your child access to any and all of this dark material. Truth is, if your child desires access to these sites, and if she is drawn to them, she will be able to find them. She is, in all likelihood, far more deft than you are at doing so. And, in my experience, kids can navigate their way around just about any "block" a parent can attempt to place in their way.

So, though I stand by any policing you choose to implement at home, I still want you to be aware, not only of the fact that this information and more is out there, but that it is readily available to your child regardless of your intervention. So, in addition to any "blocking" you may choose to implement, it is of utmost importance that you be available to talk openly with your child around these topics as well. By way of encouragement here, I find that the tipping point between a suicidal thought and a suicidal gesture is often simply a question, something along the lines of, "I notice you seem down lately. Is everything okay with you, or is there something we should be talking about?"

And you are not restricted from asking this type of question fairly frequently, as it is a matter of health and safety, physically and emotionally. Since information about mental illness is widely available and, at times, discouraging, it is imperative that you as a parent serve as a counterpoint. I do not mean to imply, by the way, that you should be trying to talk your child out of the way that she feels, even if those feelings reflect quite a bit of darkness and precious little light. Instead, you need to be available, here more than in any other part of her life, to hear her out fully, without judgment, ego, or fear. She needs to know she is not alone in her suffering. Of course, many parents feel incapable of guiding their children through this emotional landscape for a number of reasons. Perhaps we cannot relate because we have never felt this type of psychic pain ourselves. Or maybe we are overwhelmed by the idea of our child suffering or feel we are too close to the situation, too emotionally invested, to be objective and helpful.

In these circumstances, I strongly urge you to seek the help of a qualified clinician, someone with experience working with people your child's age, and with the issues she is suffering. I have had some parents express to me a feeling of failure in the fact that their child needs therapy, that they were not able to solve their issues for them on their own. I would posit that bringing your child to a therapist when it is indicated, or even *might* be indicated, is among the mightiest undertakings of loving, caring, highly effective parenting. Using all the tools at your disposal to ensure the preservation or return of your child's emotional well-being—this is excellent parenting.

All of that noted, I have a point of light to offer regarding this early awareness of mental illness. As kids talk openly with one another about their depression, their anxiety, or their therapist, the stigma that has fallen over sufferers is slowly, appropriately eroding away. And that very stigma has been an enormous, often unspoken and unrecognized part of the suffering for generations. This generation is making a difference in this regard, and supporting each other through their suffering which, I can say with some authority, has diminished that suffering quite a bit. It's a fascinating time in the history of mental illness in this regard, as celebrities from Hollywood to well-known athletes to news personalities have "come out" as sufferers of anxiety or depression. Some, like Pete Davidson of *Saturday Night Live*, find ways to inject badly needed humor into this sobering topic, which I suspect feels good to him, but it also provides the rest of us some space to do the same. I recently attended a Julia Michaels concert. If you are not familiar with her music, she writes about, and openly discusses, her struggles with anxiety and mental illness. Given the thousands in attendance, it feels like a courageous move. But she creates a literal safe space for herself and her audience and, looking around, I could see so many in the crowd find comfort in her messaging. It was a very moving experience and felt like a step squarely in the right direction in terms of removing the stigma. Now, I think it is on our generation to follow their lead and release the stigma around any mental health issues we, or our children, may be suffering.

Taking the power away from the stigma also serves to keep us out of crisis.

Your Role in Eliminating the Stigma

The last few years have truly been potent, as children and adults have realized the power they possess, on social media in particular, to do their part in eliminating the stigma and taboo affiliated with mental illness. From dedicated Instagram pages to Twitter hashtags, more and more of us are talking about our mental illnesses, how we cope, and how to provide hope for fellow sufferers. I have heard from my clients that these de facto support groups have proven invaluable in both their symptom relief and their recovery.

If you feel compelled to get involved, the National Alliance on Mental Illness (NAMI) has started an ongoing StigmaFree campaign. You, and your kids, can find details on their website, nami.org.

The Crisis Crisis

The mom was not unclear in her message: "Dr. Duffy, please call me back right away. We're really in crisis here."

There was nothing unusual about this phone call. After all, I'm a psychologist. People rarely call to let me know things are rolling along smoothly.

And this mom definitely had something salient on her mind. She had long suspected her teenage son, an honors student and accomplished athlete, had been smoking pot. But on this day, she had discovered the paraphernalia to prove herself correct:

the tiny baggies, the rolling papers, the resin-stained, trippy-colored little glass pipe.

All the signs were there. She had a major-league crisis on her hands.

But was this really a crisis, in the true sense of the word? The definition of crisis suggests an unstable, dangerous event that will dramatically impact all future events.

When I called the presumed weed smoker's mom, I asked her how she was handling the situation. She confirmed that she was in "full panic mode." In the first few minutes of the call, the subject shape-shifted from her discovery of weed in his room, to wondering whether his grades might be dropping, whether he can keep his job, whether he's hanging with the wrong crowd, whether he could still go to college, and then, "We are in a deep state of crisis here!"

There was no good available in her mind to outweigh the bad. The athlete? The honors student? The sweet kid she raised? All of that was behind her. Now there was only The Massive Weed Crisis of 2019, the dramatic, awful shift that would negatively impact everything that was to follow, the beginning of the end. The Crisis.

I am not knocking this mom. It's so very normal to feel a bit traumatized when we discover these perhaps inevitable behaviors. But take a moment and remember, this is something your kid did or tried. It's not who she *is*.

And it's likely just a situation, not a crisis.

We owe it to ourselves, and to each other, to do better. Let's agree to put an end to the Crisis Crisis. This involves thinking differently about any situation we find ourselves in with our child. Again, if we feel, and behave, as if we are in crisis, our children will respond in kind. If we use different, calmer, more empowering language, then we are modeling a method for handling situations that arise in a calm and empowering way. It is imperative that we change our thinking and behavior here and provide space for our kids to follow suit.

Creating the Un-Crisis

You may be wondering how this mom could have better reacted in this situation. After all, she did find something alarming, and some action is necessary. Well, given that we make poor decisions when we are in a crisis mindset and tend to overreact (and model overreaction in the process), the most effective thing I've witnessed is allowing the passage of a little time. I find my parent clients create far less regret for themselves when they allow even five short minutes to pass before they react. Some download the Calm or Headspace apps, and allow themselves a few minutes of meditation, a few deep breaths. Others just sit and consider the situation and their child's possible mindset. Some remind themselves that they are, in all likelihood, not suffering an actual crisis, and that they have an opportunity to create a collaborative, problem-solving atmosphere with their child, beginning now, with the situation they are dealing with.

Of course, on exceptionally rare occasion, you may find yourself dealing with an actual crisis with your child. Even in those situations, you will find that these calming, grounding techniques will provide you with the relatively calm mindset you need to engage in those few situations with grace as well.

Alcohol

It's time for us to step into some uncomfortable space here and confront some realities about our kids. The first involves drinking alcohol. And, as we will see here, in all likelihood, your child will be drinking before they are physically, emotionally, or legally prepared to do so. Knowing this, we need to make ourselves highly available to them, and keep the lines of communication with them wide open as they navigate this new frontier. And let's be honest. This is decidedly not the fun part of parenting teenagers. Our fear and anxiety in this area is legitimate, as the health and safety of our kids are at risk, no doubt. Let's walk through this together.

Unfortunately, I will not be able to cover the entire scope of drug and alcohol use and abuse by teenagers here. Honestly, the complexity of these issues, and all that is involved in them these days, is a book unto itself. My goal here is to introduce you to the methods and attitudes kids today bring to drug and alcohol use and to provide you with some guidelines on how to talk with your kids about these issues that involve their health and safety, especially given the fact that, like so much described here, exposure and use begin at startlingly early ages.

Recent studies suggest that, on average, children begin drinking alcohol between ages thirteen and fifteen. Stop and consider that for a moment. A generation ago, this age was approximately three to four years later, depending on the study cited and the population being studied. This number is also an average. It suggests, of course, that some kids do not drink until well after their fifteenth birthday. Unfortunately, on the other end, some are drinking well before they turn thirteen.

In fact, a recent study by the Foundation for Advancing Alcohol Responsibility (FAAR) has found that before eighth grade, 24 percent of children have consumed alcohol. Further, this percentage is growing year over year. And, by this time, barely 40 percent of parents have talked to their kids about alcohol. This finding puts a fine point on the assertion that we need to start the conversations early.

The urgency is clear. Young binge-drinking can lead to enormous, life-altering problems. Occurances of rape and date rape, along with other sexual assault, is exponentially more likely when alcohol is involved. High-school-age regular drinkers do more poorly in school, make maladaptive decisions, tend to participate less in extracurricular activities outside of school, and are more likely to end up in an ER. They are more likely, frankly, to become very sick or die tragically from alcohol poisoning. Also, the younger kids begin drinking, the more likely they are to become problem drinkers later in life.

Perhaps the most profound, but difficult to quantify, consequence of early drinking involves its impact on brain development. We know that parts of the brain, including the frontal lobe that allows for judgment and impulse control, are not fully developed until the mid-twenties. The risk here is significant, and far too often dismissed by our teenagers, living in the moment and feeling, well, pretty much bulletproof. The study by FAAR cited above, among abundant other research, suggests that drinking can cause substantial damage to the developing brain. Data suggests this damage can cause cognitive impairment, a breach in memory development, and potential emotional issues, among countless other neurological issues.

As with so many issues here, that initial conversation should start at eight or nine, but need not be painful. You can start with curiosity about what your child sees happening around her. What does she think about it? With this approach, you can best ensure you are engaging your child from a developmentally appropriate point of view.

As our kids get older, it's important that we nuance our approach to the alcohol discussion, as with many other topics. We tend toward an "alcohol is bad," abstinence-based approach here. This can create a disconnect for our kids, as they see and hear that alcohol provides and contributes to a lot of the joy in life. Yet we approach these topics as if the behavior is "bad," even if we are drinkers ourselves. So, our discussions need some dimension other than pure abstinence. In all likelihood, this will not be the way our children live. So, it's okay to talk about the fun of a few drinks, couched in the message that they are not ready for those drinks *right now*. Our kids are bright enough to absorb both of these messages in the same headspace.

For Generation Z kids, we do have a silver lining we can turn toward regarding alcohol use and abuse. Kids tend to do a remarkable job of taking care of one another in situations of overuse. They will tend to someone who seems ill, "out of it," or is passed out or vomiting. They are more likely than many of us were to reach out to parents or call 911 in these circumstances. They are far more likely to designate a driver, and very few ever drive drunk. So, they possess a thoughtfulness around these issues that is important and, in the extreme, may save lives. That said, they are not altogether well-informed about what might constitute problem drinking or binge drinking. So, though they are attentive, they are, on the whole, poorly informed. As we've already discussed elsewhere herein, I advocate for a high school, or perhaps even middle school, class to address the issues of mental illness and wellness, as well as drug use and abuse, for specifically these reasons.

Too often, I find that parents often have their heads in the sand when it comes to their child's drinking behavior. We are able to suggest that other children drink at young ages, but reluctant to admit to ourselves that our kids might. To punctuate this point, only about 10 percent of parents believe their teens drink, an absurdly low number given the fact that those same parents believe about 60 percent of teenagers drink overall. Further, more than half of teens openly admit to drinking alcohol. Without question, alcohol remains the substance most frequently abused by teenagers. Yet we tend to put off discussing the issue with them until it is way too late and, in many cases, we are first discussing alcohol with a child who began experimenting with it years earlier and is well into their "drinking career." Awareness is the first step to positive parenting in this regard.

The other reality we need to hold in our lens of awareness is that the clear and single largest influence on the likelihood that our children will drink is our own drinking habits. Several years ago, I worked with a family with several teenagers and young adults in the mix. The parents were my primary clients. On the whole, they had a great vibe with their children. They were connected, spent time together, and truly all enjoyed one another. But Mom was deeply concerned that Dad drank too much, recklessly and thoughtlessly, even with the kids present. She was concerned that Dad was modeling problem drinking behavior for their kids, all drinkers themselves by now. More than one of their children had been disciplined for binge-drinking, and Dad was pretty cavalier about these incidents.

But Mom pressed this issue and continued to express her concerns. Finally, Dad agreed to a series of family sessions. As it turns out, the kids were all concerned about their dad's drinking, and the session turned out to be a de facto intervention for him. Taking the cue, Dad agreed to cut back dramatically on his drinking, as long as the kids followed suit. To my surprise, after a follow-up visit a year later, the entire family found a far healthier tipping point for alcohol intake in any given day. And Dad recognized the degree to which his model drove the drinking behavior in his children, for worse and, in the end, for better.

Many parents don't believe their own behavior has such a profound impact on that of their children, but this story is no anomaly. There is no greater impact on your child's behavior than your own, in most any area of life. Our kids tend to follow our model. The more "woke" we are about this reality, the more we can consciously guide and model the behavior we want to foster, free of lectures and arguments.

All of that said, parental modeling is certainly not the sole factor in our kids' drinking behavior. Many kids drink because they feel a social pressure to drink, a pressure I have found, not incidentally, to be effectively nonexistent. Kids really do not care if their friends drink. They may gently encourage or challenge, and rarely are they comfortable being lectured by peers, but I have never worked in a situation in which a child was ostracized for abstaining. I have worked with kids who have chosen to remove themselves from drinking situations and sometimes that friend group, but rarely, if ever, are they "kicked out," even if they perceive it this way. This is no small point. Perception and reality break here, and many kids do not feel they have social permission to abstain when, in fact, they absolutely do. Non-drinkers are, in fact, highly valued among their peers. They tend to serve as the nurses and designated drivers for their drinking friends.

I personally find that kids are often looking for an excuse not to drink. In my practice, I have been asked countless times about my own drinking behavior, currently and as a teenager. The kids I work with have always been curious about that. As it happens, I have never once had a drink. More than once, I have kids come back to me suggesting they were inspired to postpone their first drink in part because I did not drink and seemed to enjoy my time nonetheless. My point here is that kids are affected by the drinking decisions of the adults surrounding them, and your behavior is paramount here. If you drink a couple glasses of wine with dinner every night and then lecture your children about the dangers of drinking, this very discerning generation will ask the obvious question.

My strong bias is to be honest with them about the answer, good and bad. With the truth on your side, your encouragement to postpone drinking will hold some water with your child. If they suspect you are posturing and behaving disingenuously, your words may mean literally nothing to them. And as with every issue we discuss here, the alcohol talk has to take place early, by the age of nine or so, maybe eight. Many parents have asked me why this is so necessary, and whether, by their bringing it up, the power of suggestion will provide their young child some kind of tacit permission to indulge in maladaptive behavior like drinking. This has not been reflective of my experience. Quite the contrary: the more kids feel they can talk openly with a parent about alcohol use, the more likely they are to both postpone initial use and to regulate far better once they are drinking.

I worked with a mom recently who came in to talk with me, ostensibly about an emergency. She reported that her sixteen-year-old son drank the night of his Homecoming dance.

Here is a reality that is difficult, understandably, for many parents to take in. In twenty-five years of practice, I have never once worked with a child who began to drink and then quit. This is one of the few Pandora's boxes of adolescence, and once open, it rarely, if ever, fully closes. The exceptions I have seen have involved either addiction, a life-threatening episode, or a long-term grounding. Otherwise, the cold reality is that kids tend to continue drinking once they begin.

This reality leaves parents with a choice to make. We can forbid our child to drink for obvious, and quite even-handed, reasons: Drinking at your age is illegal. Drinking is harmful to your developing brain. Underage drinking conflicts with my ethic and system of morality. I would feel derelict in my duty as a parent if I looked the other way and simply allowed you to drink.

Any and all of these are reasonable, and I cannot blame you for tending toward statements like these. I can also tell you, truthfully, that they are ineffective and often detrimental to your cause. If you tell your child she cannot drink once she has begun, you are effectively telling her, "You cannot talk to me about your drinking. I am an obstacle you will have to work around. And if you need me on a night when something has gone sideways with regard to you or a friend drinking, you'd best not come to me if you don't want to suffer a lecture."

This is tricky, and there is no perfect answer.

I'm asking a lot of you here, I know. I may be asking you to contravene your belief system entirely. I am absolutely not asking you, however, to condone underage drinking. You should absolutely tell your kids, in no uncertain terms, how you feel about it, including talk of the dangers affiliated with underage drinking. But in order for this discussion to be effective and to deepen your connection in a useful way, it has to be under the aegis of reality, more, "What can I do to help make sure you're safe?" than, "I forbid you."

Drugs

The nature of drug use and abuse has changed wildly in recent years, as have teenage attitudes toward drugs. We need to be very aware of the nature of drug use and how our children feel about it. As with every issue highlighted here, it is beyond critical that you not only understand what's out there and how your child feels about it (from what may feel like an uncomfortably early age) but engage in an ongoing conversation about it with your child, as well. These conversations will require a number of components, including the question of what the nature and frequency of use is in her grade, what her friends are doing, and what she herself is doing or considering doing. I fully recognize the difficult and awkward nature of engaging in these types of conversations with your children, some of whom still feel like babies to you. It is also difficult to engage your young adult children in these talks, as you may feel as if your ship of influence has already left port. But believe me, even for them, this is decidedly not the case.

Kids are aware of, and witnessing the use of, drugs of various types at all of these ages. Without question, you want your voice in the mix when they are making the tough decisions about use for themselves.

And the taboo that once existed around drug use and abuse is fading quickly, in part due to the culture of coping described above. There is also a slippery slope, I find, between the casual, presumptively cool aura of vaping and Juuling and use of other drugs. Vaping and Juuling are, in many ways, today's gateway drugs. If you are unfamiliar with these terms, vaping and Juuling, you probably come by your unfamiliarity honestly. I had never heard of them just a few short years ago. Effectively, these are covert methods for the ingestion of nicotine and marijuana, sometimes in enormous quantities.

I will remind you that nicotine is a drug, a highly addictive substance. And these devices can, and often do, contain massive quantities of the drug that will get your child hooked within weeks.

Teenagers also get very attached to the apparatus surrounding these things. The tanks, the mods, the Juul, the chargers, and the pods all have a distinctly cool vibe to them, and it takes just a moment to understand why a teenager might be drawn to them. In fact, when they acquire something new, they want to proudly show it off, sometimes to parents, often to myself. That is the degree to which these instruments carry no taboo.

Now, Juul, and many vape companies, claim their product is a smoking cessation method for adults. But make no mistake, in reality and in practice, they are highly efficient and seductive smoking starter kits for teenagers and pre-teens. And they are very effective. They are cool, and they are mechanisms for self-soothing and coping. At times, they appear reminiscent of the pacifier used by babies and toddlers. Some teenagers feel compelled to "hit" a vape or Juul, nearly unconsciously and with alarming frequency in order to cope with the moment. Now, unlike the pacifier, there is a drug involved, such that the more often you hit the vape or Juul, the more drawn to it you are. I have worked with far too many fifteen-year-olds who are troubled by their profound nicotine addiction but are not sure how they might overcome it. My office sits on the second floor, and many young people come up winded after just a few stairs, often an indication of the potency and effects of this addiction. Others have asked if they could hit their vape in the middle of a session, their last nicotine fix wearing off within the hour. It's rather alarming to witness in a child still in braces.

And the trouble with vaping doesn't stop here. I have learned, handily, that kids like to talk about vaping and Juuling, and they don't mind teaching me about it one bit. In fact, they are eager and, in fairness, they point out the flaws as well as the draws. I recently shared an hour with a seventeen-year-old boy generous enough to talk me through a typical progression. Many kids, he informed me, begin vaping and/or Juuling in middle school, often early in middle school. Some kids also use dabs, or highly concentrated wax containing THC, the active ingredient in marijuana. These tend to come in vials strikingly similar or identical to the vials of nicotine "juice" used in most vaporizers. The heating element, or mods, tend to be similar as well. The one this boy showed me was about the size of a Zippo lighter. But though one contains nicotine and the other concentrated THC, the process itself is virtually the same.

So, the use of marijuana is, behaviorally and cognitively, a short hop from vaping and Juuling. Through vaping, nicotine has become the most potent gateway drug influencing our teenagers, another perfectly legal, multi-billion-dollar, for-profit industry. The physical process is similar, and the availability of weed is almost greater, especially for kids under the legal vaping age of eighteen in most states. I asked this informative young man and several other teenage boys and girls I work with why they were drawn to vaping, Juuling, and smoking weed in all of its various methodologies. The responses were very informative and useful. Almost across the board, the answer was something along the lines of, "Life is boring. I want to feel something. I want to try something new."

If we parents need a cue toward keeping our kids occupied in positive ways, it could not be more available to us than it is right here. Please do not forget the "why" here. We have an opportunity to fill in the blanks in the lives of our kids with something far more adaptive and productive. And the window on that opportunity is, I fear, closing rather rapidly as vaping becomes more and more socially acceptable among our kids. It is rapidly becoming the norm, and the long-term negative consequences, though unclear, I suspect will prove startling.

I find the "where" to be interesting as well. These devices are far more difficult to detect than cigarettes, bongs, and joints. They are cleverly designed for stealth. It used to be, because of the visibility and odor, that kids were relegated to forest preserves, backyards, cars, and basements to ingest nicotine or marijuana. Now, I am told that, in almost any bathroom of almost any high school or middle school, even in the middle of class, you are likely to find users. You are also, to my surprise, likely to find users actually *in* class.

To prove this point to me, Grace, a high school junior, told me she would make a video, not just of her vaping in class, but of her *whole class* vaping in unison. I was pretty sure she was being superlative here. A week later, however, she proudly pulled out her phone. She showed me a video, in which she silently counts down from three and more than a dozen kids pull their sleeves up, hit their vapes, emit clouds of smoke, and draw them back in. She then turns the camera to her teacher, who turns around after writing on the board in front of the class. He clearly sees and smells nothing.

Yes, kids vape and Juul anywhere and everywhere. Even in class.

Most of these devices fit neatly up one's sleeve or in a pocket of jeans or a backpack, and because the output is vapor, it is either odorless or has a child-friendly smell that might not draw attention, like bubble gum or cereal.

Kids are strikingly casual about dealing drugs as well. Many teenagers have told me they are not drug dealers, but instead they just buy and sell for a select group of friends. The fact that this is precisely what a drug dealer does often fails to register. I have personally seen many an alarmed parent aghast to learn that their child is dealing and is nonchalant about it as well.

And it's very important to note that I am not just referencing a few kids here. I recently attended a high school class reunion. I found myself talking to one of the very few frequent pot smokers from our class. He and I tried to name everyone we could recall using drugs regularly when we were in high school. And we each came up with five names. Five names out of one thousand. Ask a teenager today what percentage of their class has tried drugs or uses them regularly, and they will tell you it is somewhere between 50 and 80 percent. So, whereas we could once easily identify those kids who were at risk, experimenting with drug use and abuse, and perhaps even had the opportunity to steer our kids clear from connection with those kids (likely a fallacy even then), this is certainly no longer the case.

For the drug dealer and the valedictorian may be one and the same. Honestly.

A few years back, not long after the advent of vaping and Juuling devices on the mass market, I noted a distinct difference between boys and girls with regard to use, with boys using far more than girls, and far more boys being regular users. I am learning quickly that this disparity is rapidly disappearing. Girls are now nearly as likely as boys to use these devices regularly.

Now, you may feel dismayed by all this new information and new delivery methods for these different types of drugs. I'll admit that, when they first arrived on the market, that's precisely how I felt. But it is important that you know what's out there, how very available it all is, and that use is rising precipitously with each passing year. And you can only help if you know and if you can talk to your kids about it. And I find that young kids are pretty dismayed and confused when these things arrive in their young lives. You need to be there to talk them through it all, and the more you come to these discussions equipped with knowledge, the better off you are.

Otherwise, I see too many parents who find themselves on "search-and-destroy" missions, going through bedrooms and backpacks seeking these tiny, stealthy devices to confront their children and destroy these items. The problem is, without discussion, nothing really changes.

The paraphernalia itself is very easily replaceable. Your connection with your child is not.

Now, aside from vaping, Juuling, and weed (discussed below), many kids use other prescription and illicit drugs, either routinely or occasionally. These can range from uppers to downers, benzodiazepines to hallucinogens. Some kids are so undiscriminating that they throw or attend the parent-horrifying, wildly dangerous and reckless Skittle parties, in which pills of all kinds are put into a bowl, and attendees take whatever they grab.

Some kids claim to be pharmaceutical experts, cautious about what they take to ensure they ingest nothing lethal, while others broadly claim not to care, a form of the passive suicidality described earlier. None of these kids could possibly know the interaction effects of one drug with another, and when multiple drugs are consumed in a night (not a rare occurrence), unanticipated ER visits are not altogether uncommon.

A former addict and current casual weed smoker I worked with recently put it well, stating, "Even I am surprised at what people are willing to put in their bodies to escape either boredom or the demons in their minds. Maybe both. I know what that pain is like, man. I've certainly been there."

Following his lead, remember that, if your child is abusing drugs of any kind, this is not an indication of the type of person they are. It is more a sign of the degree to which they need help mitigating their stress, anxiety, and depression. Heed that call. If you sense trouble in this area of your child's life, reach out to a therapist and an addictions specialist to ensure your child gains the help, medically and psychologically, that she so badly needs.

I'm Afraid My Child Has a Drug Problem

I've been on the receiving end of many calls in which a parent is deeply concerned that their child has gotten involved with drugs and may have an issue with abuse or addiction. Typically, these parents are unsure where to turn next. There are countless substance abuse and addiction resources to be found online, to help guide you through the process, especially those anxiety-filled early days. I have referred most frequently to either Rosecrance (rosecrance. org) or Hazelden (hazelden.org). Both websites provide guidelines for getting started, and counselors are available for intake and evaluation around the clock.

For more information, you can also listen to my podcast, *better.* I have interviewed a counselor with Rosecrance who talks us through the current climate of drug use and abuse among young people, as well as steps parents can take to guide their child toward recovery.

Weed

It is relevant to devote a bit of time here specifically to marijuana. First, as a parent, do not call it "marijuana," as I just did. Use your child's vernacular. Call it "weed." And if your child is inclined toward smoking it, and more and more young people are (more young men than women, though the gap is closing here too), you really need to know quite a bit about the cultural vibe surrounding weed. Again, the taboo typically affiliated with the drug is virtually nonexistent in teenagers today. I attribute this, at least in part, to the open gateways of vaping and Juuling. If you are willing to draw an illicit substance into your lungs through a device you and your peers deem cool, what's stopping you from really upping the ante and trying something that will not only get you buzzed, but is well known to achieve a high?

This generation of children holds a number of misconceptions when it comes to weed. The lecture I hear from smokers is very consistent: "It is a plant, from the *earth*. It is a far safer drug than alcohol, never taxing any of our vital organs. Nobody has every died from ingesting too much weed. Weed smokers are recreational. Drinkers are hardcore."

And so on.

Some of this may be true. A lot of it represents fallacies of convenience. First, though alcohol may be a measurably more dangerous drug, that is not evidence that weed is safe. To the contrary, weed is by far the most demotivating drug I'm aware of. If you find your child suddenly seems markedly lazy, or she is opting out of living with any degree of vigor far too often, if she is elusive, out walking the dog a lot, up in her room too much, hanging in the garage or down in the basement a suspect amount of the time, trust your suspicion, and ask the question. Weed is often the demotivating culprit.

The pot smoker and the "lazy" kid are, in my experience, often one and the same.

In fact, daily weed smoking is, to my thinking, the epitome of opting out. And the daily smoker needs to face some other realities as well. First, there is nothing at all casual about the "wake and bake," high-all-day approach to weed. If you are a daily or constant smoker, you need to face the reality that smoking is not recreational for you, not at all. Rather, smoking has become medicinal, numbing away and removing yourself from any authentic feelings—fear, anxieties, and depression—you may be suffering. Pretending anything else is folly. In fact, almost every daily, or near daily, smoker I have ever worked with admits she no longer smokes to get high or stoned, but to soothe her anxiety, manage her depression, numb her feelings about failing grades or family or social issues. Many young men have told me they smoke daily but primarily at night. In order to fall asleep. Upon reflection, many of them have experienced too much existential pain to allow them peace of mind, so they medicate consciousness away.

Come to think of it, this is what frequent smokers do when they are awake as well. Weed is a very effective escape from one's own psyche.

The risk is losing out on large swaths of one's life. I recent reconnected with Timothy, a young man I had initially worked with in his late teens. Then, he was a brilliant, burgeoning musician, but he was haunted by some sexual abuse in his earlier years and was deeply self-critical and self-loathing as a result.

Within a few months, he discontinued therapy without ever fully resolving these deep-seated issues. A full ten years later, he reached out asking to reconnect and begin therapy anew. I always find calls like this quite heartening. Sometimes, young people are simply not in the emotional space to engage in a course of therapy. Hearing back from them when finally they are ready, and the speed with which they make progress in that second round, is heartwarming.

A decade on, Timothy surprised me. Excited to see him, I stepped into the hall to greet him. And honestly, I did not recognize him, even remotely, a rarity for me. He was a full hundred pounds heavier than he had been a decade earlier. He moved slowly, as if he were far older than his twenty-nine years. His face was drawn and sallow, his clothing enormous and shapeless.

As he approached, the stench of weed surrounding him was overwhelming.

And he knew. He knew all of it. He reported that he had spent the past decade in his mother's basement, smoking weed many times a day. Occasionally, he would get a job as a barista or a barback, but these tended not to last. Sometimes, he would fail a mandatory drug test and lose the job. Sometimes, he would sleep in and skip a shift. A couple times, he just stopped showing up, ignoring calls and retreating onto the basement couch in a thin cloud of fetid smoke.

The story he had to tell me of his "lost decade" was a grim one. He had made no friends, been on no dates, completed not a single class (after achieving a 35 on the ACT, nearly perfect, no less). Looking back, he feels he never really grieved the loss of his father years ago or some family-related trauma from his childhood. Instead, he self-medicated. And he did not drink. He never ingested harder drugs. He smoked weed.

Weed is dangerous, period. It may not kill you literally, but Timothy might well argue that it can take many years of your life figuratively, and that any memories of those years may well be erased as well, another potent side effect of THC in excess. No drug drains motivation and spark with the facility of frequent, prolonged weed use. And Timothy will tell, with great sadness, that the loss of time and potential and connection could never, ever be worth the disappearing act of weed.

There are a few other pertinent facts about this drug you need to be aware of. First, based on your own experiences or what you witnessed back in your teenage days, you may envision that weed is smoked through bowls, joints, bongs, and blunts. This remains true to this day. On the market now, however, are myriad other methods for ingesting weed, each of them offering different concentrations, dosages, and alleged symptom relief.

Weed can be vaped and Juuled, as we have pointed out. It can also be baked into brownies or other "edibles," or distilled into wax-like dabs, and even lollipops. Yep.

You may also think that weed today bears some resemblance to the weed you or your friends may have smoked or experimented with back in high school. But man, is it ever different. The CDC reports that some of the most commonly used strains of weed are as much as twenty to thirty times higher in THC than the drug was thirty years back. That's no small change. That is, in effect, a different drug altogether. It is wildly more potent and addictive, physically or, at the very least, mentally, today than it was then. Again, I work with some kids who feel they cannot go to sleep without smoking.

Weed is also notoriously easy for your kids to acquire today. Ask the most straight-edge teenager where you can get weed within the hour (something I have asked dozens of them), and they will know dealer names and cell numbers and houses. And the distribution channels are pretty clean. Rare is the child who is heading into the bowels of the inner city to buy from a "criminal element" and put themselves in apparent harm's way. Weed is far more likely to be bought and sold in the halls and bathrooms of high schools and middle schools, or in the basements of houses like yours.

The key is not only to determine the reasons your child chooses to smoke, but for *them* to recognize and integrate those reasons. This is the more difficult part, to be sure. And in my experience, the only way to achieve this formidable goal is to get your child talking, openly, about her use and abuse of the drug.

The tendency here for parents, far too often, is to focus on the behavior we find unacceptable. Again, if we follow this approach, we inevitably end up in a debate about the merits of weed relative to other drugs: alcohol, heroin, meth, and on and on. There is nether merit nor end point in this type of argument. Instead, focus on the *why*. Why does she smoke so frequently? What feelings does the drug protect her from? How else might she cope?

By way of example, I need to walk you through an alarming new weed-related trend I've been seeing in the last couple of years.

When I met him, Bill was an eighteen-year-old, high-functioning college freshman. He had recently visited a high school friend at another college, and they smoked weed, not much, pretty casually. By the next morning, Bill felt as if something were terribly wrong with him. He felt disoriented, cognitively "fuzzy," and bizarre. This intense feeling lasted through the next several weeks. By the time he landed on my couch, he had been to the ER twice and had rejected two other therapists who said nothing was wrong with him.

And the truth is, after sitting with him for an hour, it was clear to me that nothing *was* wrong with him. He communicated well, expressed appropriate affect, and even showed a bit of a sense of humor. But he continued to feel as if he had done some irreparable damage to his mind, a direct result of that night of smoking. Filled with anxiety about this situation, he sought out a CT scan and an MRI, hoping they would find a lesion or a tumor, something that would explain his feelings of "psychosis." To his horror, the tests were clean.

This nightmarish situation lasted about six months for Bill. Only then did he feel he had some control over his mind and recognize that he had gotten past this situation.

I would like to report that this was an isolated incident. But I have worked with nearly a dozen young men who have told me virtually the identical story and suffered the same symptoms as Bill for months. All very smart, high-functioning, motivated guys. I share a group text with a number of other therapists. We recently realized that we had all treated young people who had experienced an episode of smoking weed, followed by a period when they felt as if they were psychotic, like Bill.

The causes of this phenomenon remain unclear. We have considered the possibility that, because the strength and potency of THC is very difficult to dose, these episodes are a function of something akin to overdose. This happens frequently with edibles, for example, as kids will often eat more and more if they do not experience the effect of being high rather quickly, only to be vomiting an hour later because they have ingested more THC than their system can handle.

Of course, it is also highly possible that the weed a child is smoking is laced with some other drug, and nearly any other drug is possible. As it is illegal in most states, weed is wholly unregulated. Therefore, in order to get our kids hooked on a more expensive, more addictive substance, dealers will often lace the weed they sell with something more dangerous and lethal to our kids, heroin, meth, LSD, or PCP, to name a few. This is always a risk, even if your child buys from a friend, even if it's the same friend every time. This is a real risk to your child's health and safety, and you need to be aware of it.

Objectively, by the way, I have never found that there was anything whatsoever wrong with the brain of someone who had experienced a "bad trip." Not once. But that doesn't quell their concerns at all. Imagine feeling as if you had made one mistake one night that seems to have permanently altered your brain, disconnecting you from normal thought, brain function, and joy.

As you might guess, over the weeks and months, hopelessness tends to set in. Hospitalization, or at the very least, intensive therapy, is required to ensure the patient stays well enough through the process of recovery.

And the good news is that I have never worked with anyone who did not recover, fully, from such an episode. The residual guilt and regret often lingers, however. And there is often a mess to clean up: a semester lost, friendships strained, family relationships in turmoil after the prolonged crisis, and, of course, the fear that the feeling may return.

Weed is not without its risks, and some people pay a very large price for smoking.

Now, many young people smoke pot without running into the type of life-altering, in fact life-draining, difficulties that Bill ran into. For many, smoking is a relatively infrequent social experience. This presentation offers parents a different type of challenge. Here we have a drug, illegal in some states but fully legal in others, used in relative moderation in a social setting.

Bottom line: kids *keep* it moderate when they can talk to their parents about it.

So, you want to make sure your voice is clearly in the mix when your child is making decisions regarding drug usage, including smoking weed. And, in my seasoned opinion, you would rather know than not know. A "don't ask, don't tell" policy is a foolhardy cat-and-mouse game when played out within a family, fostering furtive secrets and eroding trust, trust that tends to diminish not in just this one area of life, but potentially in many other areas as well. The tradeoff is simply not worth it.

It is also important to note that the fact that your child smokes does not fundamentally change their nature. This may not have been entirely true a generation ago, but, today, good kids smoke. It is not just the sorry end of the bell curve wasted in the bathroom during class. Weed smokers are honor roll students and athletes and actors and cheerleaders. Do not judge your child based on this behavior alone.

Finally, it is relevant to note here that the culture around weed is changing rapidly, as we all know. Each year, more states legalize weed, such that there are fully legal dispensaries scattered across the country, with weed as available to the consumer as a decaf latte. This newly emboldened presence is inevitably going to increase usage and bolster the thinking that weed brings no downside for the user. Remember that this is not true.

Prescription Drugs

Not only are kids today familiar with the full menu of mental and emotional diagnoses that may befall them or their peers, they are also quite aware of the panoply of drugs available to treat these issues. In my experience, this awareness, the frequency with which they are discussed and dispensed, and the ready availability of far too many of these psychotropic medications makes far too many kids suggestible, questioning whether they lack the resilience to manage their lives without medication. More and more kids are on medications for depression and anxiety than ever before, for instance. And I can attest firsthand, despite the fact that I have no prescription authority, that many of them do not truly *need* the medications they take.

This is most true of kids medicated for ADHD. There is definitely a small subset of children who truly suffer from attention issues so profound that a prescription for Adderall, Ritalin, or Focalin may prove helpful for them to function. But I find that these meds are often prescribed upon request, with just the suggestion of ordinary difficulty in focus and concentration. The behavior being addressed, by the way, tends to be descriptive of teen and pre-teen boys on the whole, who naturally idle on high. And make no mistake, the majority of these prescriptions are specifically disempowering to kids, suggesting clearly that they cannot manage their world without the medication. With this belief system in place, just imagine how difficult it must be for a child to remove herself from any of these medications, while simultaneously fearing she may not be able to make it adequately through her days without enormous strain and suffering.

Further, many teenagers can be, understandably, quite suggestible in this regard. They hear about psychiatric diagnoses and psychotropic medications from peers, and the degree to which these peers feel they need to rely on them. For many kids, this begs an almost immediate question: "Do I suffer the same condition? If she cannot manage the stressors of the world around her without medication and a diagnosis, can I? Perhaps I am suffering from a mental illness too." The result too often is that a perfectly resilient child questions her own ability to get along unassisted and a presumption of dependency is too often the result.

For many groups of teenagers, there is a stealth element of social pressure that applies here as well. For these growing subgroups, depression, anxiety, and suffering in general suggest a certain depth, wisdom, degree of character, empathy, and a connection through suffering. The idea here is that the sufferer possesses a keener, deeper understanding of the human condition. I have worked with more than one teenager who wonders whether she is adequate if she is not suffering *enough*. This twisted logic can lead our kids directly into romanticizing psychological suffering and often even thoughts of suicide and suicidal ideation.

As parents, we have an emotional needle to thread. First, we need to listen, fully and completely, without agenda and, to the extent we can, without fear. We have to be prepared for the very real possibility that, should our kids open up to us, we may not be entirely pleased or comforted by the things they have to say about their emotional well-being. But we need to listen, non-judgmentally, regardless. Only when our kids feel heard, truly heard, can we offer our thoughts and opinions. We need to open a dialogue with them, one that will be open and ongoing. They need to know that we are available to be their go-to when they have thoughts or questions about their emotional life. By the way, I am fully aware that these themes are repetitive here. That is precisely my intention. The openness and connection are so crucial to your child's ongoing emotional well-being, and you are the stewards of that well-being.

We can also weigh in. If we have more faith in our child's resilience than she does, it is important that we say so and delineate why. It is important to note that we must be genuine with our kids today—open and real and honest. They are excellent BS detectors, something I believe serves them, and will continue to serve them, quite well in their lives. They will know if you are patronizing them or vilifying them. Speak your truth with them. They are, in all likelihood, far more grown up, thoughtful, and intelligent then you think they might be. Do not underestimate any of that. And they need you and your sincerity more than any generation of teenagers have needed their parents, ever. Their "teenage" lives are starting too early, and we need to buoy them, not with pabulum, but with sincerity and kindness and yes, unconditional positive regard.

The Opioid Crisis

Never before have we culturally witnessed a drug crisis as severe as the opioid issue confronting our nation right now. I have personally not only treated addicts and recovering addicts, but I have read countless journal and magazine articles attempting to gain purchase on the causes, nature of, and solutions to this crisis. In short, years ago, one family came up with a single drug, OxyContin, pitched as a merciful approach to managing the enormous pain suffered by terminal cancer patients. Morphine, it was argued, was simply not doing the trick.

Well aware that this was a highly addictive substance, but having acquired full FDA approval, the network of pharmaceutical organizations ensured that doctors prescribed enormous quantities of these pills in excessive doses. Opioids quickly became a silent, precious industry worth billions. In terms of the neurochemistry, Oxy and heroin were virtually indistinguishable, by the way. A crisis of addiction was all but inevitable.

Now, you may suspect that you can skip this section of the text or wonder why it is included in the first place. You may feel certain your child is innocent and resilient enough that, at the least, she is culturally inoculated from opioid addiction.

Don't be so sure.

Any profile you put on the opioid addict is likely a dubious and inaccurate one. So many of these addictions start with pain, often due to some injury or other, often a sports injury. One young woman I worked with was prescribed opiate medication for headaches she had been suffering. Within a few months, she reports, she was addicted, high every waking moment, and mostly unaware of the passage of time.

Now, some people become addicted to opioids for the same reason others become addicted to heroin, meth, or other drugs. They are spiritually broken, and this is their only way of coping, in their eyes, while still drawing breath. More than one addict has described this process to me as suicide, but over the course of months and years rather than in a snap-decision moment. But others come by their addiction quite by accident, their worst years coming in the wake of an injury and following doctor's orders.

I think we need to seriously revisit the nature of these alleged medications and whether they belong on the market at all. The FDA also needs to take a far deeper look into the nature of the prescriptions and the profit model that drives them. This is true, by the way, not only of the opiates, but also of the benzodiazepines and other addictive substances, especially those that seem to particularly appeal to our young people.

Because of the dangers these drugs can present, talk with your child's prescribing doctor about the risks before administering opioids or benzodiazepines to your child. And be sure to dispense them to your child yourself. Also, be aware of any addictive medications you yourself may be prescribed. I find that kids are pretty well aware of your medicine cabinet or bedside drawer. If you complete a course of treatment, I strongly encourage you, for the sake of safety, to dispose of unused medication.

Video Games

Man, do we parents loathe video games, am I right? We feel they are a colossal waste of time. They are disconnecting. They are violent and promote violent tendencies. Just the sight of the controller is enough to make us furious, typically with our sons. And there is almost always a video game *du jour*, a favorite amongst teenage boys and young men and a group of girls and young women.

Like the makers of vapes and Juuls, the designers of video games are clever. They are experts at drawing kids in and holding their attention. Somewhere in those programming psyches, they must be aware of the fact that our kids carry a lot of anxiety and are prone to distraction. The properly designed video games fit the curative bill surprisingly well.

Years ago, interactive games like *Halo* drew attention from some kids for a few months at a time. Then, more profane, violent games like *Grand Theft Auto*, games that filled the screen with chaos and required lightning-quick reflexes to remain alive and well in the game, took center stage. When smartphones were released, sophisticated games came along for the ride, stranding kids in backseats of cars everywhere whiling away time, heads down. For a moment, a few years ago, *Pokémon Go* captured the minds of kids, adding an element of movement that I, for one, appreciated for obvious reasons. If you're going to play a game, I'd rather you *actually* walk around a bit to capture a Pikachu. In a little way, you earned that Pokémon. And the modicum of exercise involved was better than nothing.

Fortnite is the game that has taken over lately. Recognizing the short attention span of most of us, the crafters of this game decided to make each battle brief, thirty to forty minutes or so. As opposed to "leveling up" in games that can take weeks or even months to complete, you can play several games of *Fortnite* in a single sitting. I suspect the designers were familiar with the intermittent reinforcement found in casinos and played off that concept in drawing kids in to *Fortnite*. The struggle for most parents is pulling kids away from it, as they insist one more battle will only take a few minutes.

I'll be morbidly interested in seeing what ploy this industry will tap next to engage our disengaged kids. Because you should know that games are introduced to the market in a staggered model, so that once a teenager tires of one, the next is ready for release. This way, several games can be released annually, keeping our disengaged kids fully engaged, and quietly creating an industry that dwarfs Hollywood.

No doubt, the next *Fortnite* is in the hopper.

If you suspect there is a significant problem brewing here, you are correct. The American Psychiatric Association is in the process of allowing some form of Video Game Addiction into the next edition of the *Diagnostic and Statistical Manual of Mental Disorders (DSM-6)*. Over the years, I admit I have balked at the use of the addiction model for something external like a video game. But when you investigate the ways in which games play on the neurochemistry of the brain, man, does it ever look like addiction. And many of you parents can testify that, behaviorally, it feels an awful lot like addiction.

The question rapidly becomes, "What do we do about our addicted gamers?"

And that's why we're here. Many of us, myself included, I suppose, would love to go back in time and eradicate this video gaming craze altogether. Alas, this is not an option. What we can do is push gaming to the margins of our kids' lives, instead of allowing it to occupy hours of their days. Remember, any more than two hours of screen time a day, time spent on *any* screen, can produce a marked rise in anxiety, depression, attention issues, and even suicidal ideation. That is, we cannot afford the luxury of ignoring this issue. If it cannot be eliminated, it needs to be, at the very least, controlled. And I find video games to be particularly agitating, anxiety-inducing, and depressing, even relative to other screens. In my experience, some kids get quite down on themselves if they are not expert in their game of choice, such that (and I'm not kidding here) self-esteem can take a dramatic hit.

If you have younger children, of course, you can start by capping time limits, getting your child accustomed to self-regulation, playing for just a while, then moving on to some other activity. If your child is as old as ten or so, however, that ship has likely already long since sailed. I conceptualize gaming the same way I think of other vices our kids are presented with, whether it be their phone or a Juul, smoking weed or Snapchat. If they are living a full life, then these elements remain in the fringes, occupying bits and pieces of their days and nights. But if the lens is permanently fixed on any of them through countless hours, that is troubling.

As parents, however, we tend to focus our own lenses incorrectly as well. Naturally, we strive to manage the gaming behavior, lecturing our kids about how unhealthy it can be. Inevitably, arguments ensue, typically with unsatisfactory resolutions. I have yet to talk with a family who worked out this whole gaming issue through a screaming contest. But that doesn't stop us from engaging in them. Instead, I strongly suggest, once again, filling in the spaces around gaming. Make sure your child is involved in something extracurricular. Make sure she is moving and otherwise engaged, a *lot* of the time. Gaming is too easy a time-filling default otherwise.

Now, inherent in this recommendation lies the fact that I think most of us need to accept that our child will be drawn to games sometimes. This is part of the culture they have inherited. Again, none of this was their idea. None of it is their fault. As far as they are concerned, it has always been this way.

Think about it. It has.

The Upside of Gaming

Playing the contrarian to my own point of view, gaming in and of itself is not all bad. Watch your child play sometime. The speed and dexterity required to play successfully is pretty impressive. The attention required to do well is equally striking. And if a game is interactive, there is a true social component to it. Many kids are talking and laughing while playing, with the game itself in the margins. It is a social outlet for many kids, and some of my more introverted clients often feel gaming threads the needle between direct social contact and loneliness and isolation.

Relationships and Sex

Relationships for kids today are murkier than perhaps they have ever been. Kids tend to hang out in groups, sometimes co-ed, sometimes not. Though they feel longings and crushes for one another like we did, the language and the way it all plays out are entirely different. Sometimes a couple will break off from the larger group and date, and that is considered, relatively speaking, fairly serious. Other times, a couple will break off partially from the group, "talk" more online and in person, and "hook up," either frequently or on occasion.

The language used here is confusing, as you likely know. Ask a dozen teenagers, boys and girls alike, what "hooking up" specifically means, and the answers will run the gamut from making out to intercourse, and everything and anything in between. The same goes, believe it or not, for the word "talking," I have learned. Many kids describe the early stages of relationships with this word. Others describe talking as a pre-sexual relationship, or one that has not yet led to sex. It's not unimportant to talk with your kids about the meaning of these terms among themselves and their peers. I have found that kids can feel as confused by the multiple meanings, and what is expected of them, as their parents do.

Regardless, it is important to note that these early relationships are very important to teenagers. I would not dismiss them as frivolous or meaningless—just recall how important your first crushes and relationships were to you. For kids today, these early relationships set the tone and tenor for future relationships, without a doubt. This is why your model, early on, is so critically important. Second, many kids steady themselves emotionally through these relationships. They lean on their current significant others during difficult times and celebrate their victories with them. And I find that, regardless of what any of them might tell you about their desire for the hookup culture and how fun and carefree it can be, kids *want* to be in relationships for these reasons. They do not want to engage in the random hookups. They are aware of the disconnect of hooking up without any deeper relationship.

Still, your child may very well be engaging in just this type of physical relationship regularly—an awful lot of kids are.

But the hookup culture is neither good for their well-being, nor for their long view of relationships. Frankly, I do find social media to be, at least in part, responsible for the hookup culture that has evolved among teens over the last decade or so. Both girls and boys often report to one another whether they hooked up at a party, for example. This is part of the metric of belonging, having fun, and being a part of the popular crowd that social media tends to foster. It's quite an impersonal, somewhat joyless process, and kids report to me that they are keenly aware of this reality. But the sense of needing to keep up trumps all of this.

There are, of course, significant risks affiliated with the hookup culture. The risk of pregnancy, sexually transmitted diseases, and sexual violence (more on this below) are all far greater with random hookups. Further, the risk is exacerbated by the fact that our kids are often intoxicated, on some substance or other, when they are involved. In order to best inoculate your child from this, I believe a couple of important interventions are necessary from you as the parent.

First, as you might guess by now, you need to communicate openly about sex and hooking up with your teen. Your parents may not have engaged in much of a sex talk with you—I know mine never broached the subject even remotely. But, as you are reading here, ignoring the talk about sex is simply not an option for parents today. We need to talk to our kids, considering their age, maturity, and developmental level, and express our feelings about their readiness, respect for others, and respect for their own bodies, clearly and relatively frequently. That's the talking part.

But most importantly, we need to draw our kids out on this subject, and we need to listen. This requires an unprecedented sense of openness and availability from you. Here, you need to make the uncomfortable far more comfortable. And trust me, the primary source of discomfort around this topic, in all likelihood, resides in *you*. So, you need to find your comfort zone, quickly and early in your child's life, in order to guide her here, and help her navigate her own feelings about sex, and hooking up, about love and crushes and relationships. In order for her to feel comfortable being open and honest with you, you need to set the tone here. It requires you to approach the topic gently, gingerly, briefly (neither of you will want to talk for hours on this), and often.

You, for one, will feel far better knowing the line of communication between you is open regarding sex and sexuality. And though she may never point it out to you, she will be grateful for that openness as well.

Parents express more reluctance and queasiness in the area of sexual activity than any other. Specifically, I am asked if parents can, at the least, postpone the sex talk until their child is closer to the teen years, as it feels odd and uncomfortable talking to your pre-teen about these things. It's awkward enough to talk to your *actual* teen about it. But here's an issue where it's critical to reflect for a moment on the massive cultural shift we've seen. It has impacted sexual activity among very young children as much as, or more than, any other area. For instance, across the US, approximately 8 percent of boys are having sex before their thirteenth birthday, according to a new study by the JAMA (Journal of the American Medical Association) Pediatrics. Further, the percentage is substantially higher, and the age younger, in some geographic areas than others. And the trend suggests more children having sex, and engaging in various sexual activities, at younger and younger ages. So, the talk has to begin young, again, with questions and curiosity. After all, there's no need to expose our young children to too much too soon. And many of my clients have suggested to me that the current hookup culture exerts some peer pressure to engage in sexual activity earlier and earlier, whether that pressure is actual or simply perceived.

Now, despite the prominence of the hookup culture, I will remind you that, in the sanctity and anonymity of the therapy room, none of it holds any appeal to kids. They describe it alternately as vulgar, disconnecting, anxiety-provoking, and depressing. But they are deeply ensconced within it nonetheless. In the end, however, I find teenagers, like the rest of us, want someone that they can care for and take care of, and vice versa. Curiously, though I hear this sentiment from both genders, I hear it far more often from boys than girls.

Also, boys are far more open and vulnerable in therapy, of course, than they are out in the "real world." And I worry that we may be fostering something in them culturally, defining masculinity for them in such a way that they feel a need to keep their true gentleness and vulnerability hidden, under wraps. A few years ago, I interviewed a group of boys about sex and sexuality for a television talk show. These were sweet, polite, open, articulate, and intelligent teenage boys. And they knew their comments would be televised for everyone, even their parents, to see. Yet still, they described girls as conquests and sexual favors from girls in ways that surprised and alarmed even me. If we collectively continue to further the toxicity of the "alpha male" narrative, we are continuing to cocreate complicated, perhaps even dangerous, relationship dynamics for both boys and girls going forward.

A lot of relationship time between teenagers today, even in rather serious relationships, takes place via texting, Snapchat, and FaceTime. In moderation, I think this is perfectly fine. But only in moderation. Who wouldn't want to talk with and connect with their girlfriend or boyfriend at any time? There is a solid argument to be made that this relatively new dynamic offers a tendency to bring a couple closer, and to talk and get to know one another better, than the constant sexual pressure when they are together physically. Teenage couples today, I would argue, actually talk and write to one another far more than we did a generation ago. They know their partner's point of view, and they know it well. They share how they feel about one another, openly and honestly, quite frequently. Given that this technology will not be going away in their lifetimes but is likely to amplify in ways we cannot even imagine in this moment, I think this methodology provides a good template for the way kids will connect with their partners as adults.

This part I like, a lot.

The other good news is that dating and connecting is far more egalitarian than it has been in the past. Kids tell me is it becoming equally acceptable for a girl to reach out to a guy as the reverse, though the initial contact may very well take place via text. If you lament the fact that the anxious butterflies of asking someone out, in person, while navigating her parents and the phone and everything else, is missing, you are not alone. But we all need to remember, none of this was your child's idea. And as far as she's concerned, this is the way it has always been.

Regardless, I think we want to see our children in relationships, at least some of the time. First, it's fun and exciting for them, one of the true adolescent rites of passage. But it's also important for them to learn to navigate this type of emotional connection while under your roof, so that you can be available to them in real time. Don't forget that, inevitably, these early relationships tend not to last. You want to be there, present and available, for the heartbreak and fallout of the breakup, which can feel quite devastating, we all know, in real time.

We all hate the idea that our kids are sexualized and are introduced to sexual material and their own sexuality very early in their lives. But again, this is a reality we must realize and accept, so that we can talk openly about it and prepare our kids for it. In no area is this more apparent, or more awkward, than it is around the topic of pornography.

Pornography is a major player in the way our kids view sexuality. Again, kids are exposed to pornographic material far too early in their lives, well before their young minds can assimilate the images they are confronted with. They typically come across it innocently online, at first. But I have worked with kids, primarily boys, who, left unmonitored, become addicted to pornography much like the addiction to video games we discussed earlier, with several pleasure centers of the brain all activated simultaneously. It's a pretty powerful draw.

It also concerns me greatly as a therapist, as it provides kids with such a broadly skewed view of sexuality, what it should look like, and what it should feel like. The dehumanizing of women and the sexual violence often depicted within pornographic material can connect with a suggestibility in the already wounded teen, or someone who was sexually abused early in life, that truly alarms me. An uncanny number of boys and young men have come to my office in recent years complaining of sexual performance anxiety, much of it driven by pornography. It is difficult to convince young men that the sex they see played out in a pornographic scene is just that, a scene, acted out. The insecurity these boys and young men suffer as a result can be quite crippling, sexually and socially. In my experience, a course in therapy, with a therapist comfortable with these issues, is the most salient remedy.

We need to talk with our kids, frequently, about relationships, sex, sexuality, and pornography. If you are looking for opportunity, I highly recommend judicious use of the Pause button on the TV. Sit and watch with your child for a while. Regardless of what's on, I suspect you will find some kind of sexual material shows up within minutes. Just hit Pause, and note that you are about engage in another awkward, albeit brief, discussion about relationships or sex.

Then, hit the Play button and move on. Provided you are truly ready for this to be an ongoing discussion, you will have more opportunities. And then, when your child is making those tough calls, those talks will be in her head. If she feels a need for counsel, you are setting the stage beautifully for her to come to you. This may be a tad uncomfortable, but I assure you it's the vibe you want to carry with your child. You will feel more connected, worry far less, and she may well be safer, emotionally and otherwise, with you in her corner as an ally, guide, and consultant.

Before moving on, we do need to address sexting. Ew, right?

By definition, if you find yourself unfamiliar, sexting is the sending of sexually explicit material (naked selfies, texts, graphically suggestive memes) to one another. Sometimes, sexting involves requesting a specific sexual act. I can tell you unequivocally that parents who stumble across sexting on their child's phone, via Snapchat, text, or some other medium, are alarmed, at what their child is not only aware of, but actively engaged in. It is a new and unfamiliar trauma, and the associated shame often feels as if it permeates an entire family.

And stepping out of my clinical shoes for just a moment here, in fairness to any parent who has or will come across it, sexting *from* your child is typically awful, simply mortifying to stumble upon. And it does make a parent, understandably, feel as if they have been missing the bigger picture of their child's life and that there is this festering wretchedness that has somehow eluded them altogether.

Far too often, parents judge themselves when they find that their child has been sexting.

We also feel taken quite far aback. How does she even know what that act is? Why would she ever negotiate with someone about whether to do it? Doesn't she have more pride in herself than that? Have I taught her nothing in the way of values and morals?

I totally get it. This is a parental trauma, and, if you have been there, I feel awful about that. Too often, I have seen the pained, terrified, disempowered look in the face of a mom or dad who has found this stuff. Some fear they are raising sexual deviants who may be hopeless. Others feel as if they have erred in their own self-assessment of their parenting acumen.

I worked recently with a seventh-grade girl who talked about the nude selfies her friends were sending to boys in their class. She was in therapy because she was being shamed for *not* sending naked pictures of herself. I know. It's awful. But it is the reality of our kids' lives today.

So, as a mighty parent, I need to ask you to set your judgment aside, of both yourself and your child, and make yourself fully available to talk to your kids. Approach the edges of the topic with them. Ask broad, open-ended questions. Open the door to the discussion, and let them lead the way. If you've got a substantial balance in the Emotional Bank Account, you may find this to be an easier discussion than you think.

And in doing so, you will be helping her clarify her own points of view on some of these topics, thinking before she does anything in this area. Man, that is invaluable, right? You may spare her some mortifying, even dangerous, times herself.

Resources for You

Talking about sex and sexuality can be so very uncomfortable, and I have worked with some parents who have said that, since they were never privy to this talk from their own parents, they would benefit from either a starter kit or a refresher course. To that end, I highly recommend reading either *s.e.x. the all-you-need-to-know sexuality guide to get you through your teens and twenties* by Heather Corinna or *Making Sense of It: A Guide to Sex for Teens (and Their Parents too!)* by Alison Macklin.

Sexual Identity and Orientation

More and more teens are coming out, at earlier and earlier ages, than ever before. Often, they come out to their peers before their parents and family, as many have told me they find their peers to be more broadly accepting and understanding and fully supportive. These tend to be discussions we don't expect or, if we do, that many of us dread. Some parents, I find, are mortified by the fact that their child is gay and wish it away as a phase caused by the power of suggestion from peers. Other parents worry about the lives their children will have to lead, the difficulties and biases they will undoubtedly face. And many wonder how their child, at fifteen, or thirteen, or eleven, could possibly even *know* their sexual identity.

I find that parents are often baffled by the myriad sexual-identity-related labels as well. You may hear children with gender identities as varied as straight, gay, lesbian, bisexual, pansexual, queer, and so on. Surely, we think, our kids are trying these "new" identities on to determine what feels most authentic to them, and they will land somewhere in the mainstream in the final determination.

After years of working with kids struggling through issues of sexual identity, I find that this is rarely if ever the case, reads as wishful thinking by parents, and feels like flat-out rejection to our children.

There are a number of points here I know to be true. First, your child is, in all likelihood, far more comfortable with issues of sexuality and sexual identity than you can imagine. Whether we like it or not, prefer it or not, value it or not, they are presented with sexual thinking and material early in life. It is a part of their vernacular, and they possess a more healthy, open approach, I find, to discussing these issues than their parents.

Because they are aware of sexuality at earlier ages, they are aware of themselves as sexual beings from a young age as well. So, they therefore consider their sexuality in ways we may never have, and certainly earlier than we ever did. That's one of the reasons I believe many kids are more aware of their sexual identities at a young age. And frankly, the cultural atmosphere of your child's generation is far more open and accepting than we were a generation ago. With regard to sexual identity, most of them are quite matter-of-fact about it. I find this to be an encouraging shift in the tide. It's safer to come out now, a lot safer.

And if your child tells you she is gay, or straight, or queer, believe her. Hold her. Embrace all that she is. There is enormous courage and vulnerability, and fear and anxiety, involved in coming out to parents. This is an issue; kids tend to suffer in fear, often for months, more often for years. But her wellness is certainly at risk. For instance, the CDC recently completed research suggesting that approximately half of all transgender youth are at risk for significant mental and emotional health difficulties, as well as suicidality. This group is far more likely to be bullied, suffer violence (sexual and otherwise), and abuse drugs and alcohol as well. So, her fear outweighs yours by a significant margin, and the impact on her life trumps the impact on yours. Your job must be to support her, wholly and unconditionally. After all, she is the child you have raised and loved to this point. The announcement of her sexual identity should make no difference whatsoever.

I impress this so strongly for a few reasons, the most important of which is the impact of sexual identity, and the suppression of it, on mental health and well-being. The rate of depression, suicidal ideation, and completed suicide among the LGBTQ community is far greater than the rates in the society as a whole. These groups, and they are separate and distinct groups, are far too often marginalized, not just within cultures, but within households. That is to say, your child's emotional well-being may well hinge, to a great extent, on your radical acceptance in this area of her life. This is no small thing.

All of that said, I am quite familiar with the shock waves that a child's sexual identity, outside the norm, can send through families. Parents and siblings often feel as if they suddenly have no idea what to say, how to behave, or even how to address this person they thought they knew so intimately before the announcement. I get it. A different sexual identity than expected changes a lot and can generate a lot of anxiety. I get it. And so many questions undoubtedly arise. Do we know how to raise a gay child? Will our queer child be ostracized? Will he or she enjoy their life? Have a family? Find someone to love them?

I get it.

My bias is to recognize that there is a process here, and a difference between acceptance and assimilation. That is, we need to accept our child as she is, regardless of sexual identity, right now. Once that is clear, the process begins of assimilating this new information into your family. This requires discussions and questions, some of which our child undoubtedly will not be able to answer, especially at first.

There is, or certainly can be, joy and connection and laughter in that. Trust me here. The alternative is that you are left in the cold, removed from your child's life because of your own insecurity and discomfort. In the long game, you will be the one left behind. Your child will move on with her life, assimilate her sexual identity into her overall identity, find love and joy and make connections. You will simply not be a part of it. Trust me on this. I have worked with parents who recognized too late that their rejection drove their now-adult son's rejection of them. When he married, they were not welcome. They do not know their two grandchildren. And they would do anything to go back in time and undo the damage.

The better story here is obvious. And if you find yourself struggling to find that note of acceptance, if you find you have a mental, or religious, or moral, or fear-based block to your child's sexual identity, do not ignore the dissonance. Instead, find a therapist with experience in this area. Seek the guidance that will help you maintain the critical connection with your child at a critical time in her life.

Sexual Assault

Given the nature of the headlines over the past several years, your children are also keenly aware of the nature and frequency of sexual assault in our culture. Like sex and sexual identity, this also must be an open topic for discussion with your child, never a taboo. Recently, I found myself trying to tabulate the number of teenage girls and young women I have worked with over the years who have been sexually assaulted in some way. Many faces and names passed through my mind, but the number is unclear to me: certainly many dozens, perhaps hundreds. I have also, not incidentally, worked with many teenage boys and young men who have been sexually assaulted as well. That said, it is noteworthy that every assault that has been reported to me, every single one, was perpetrated by a boy or a man. Collectively, we clearly need to do better for the sake of both our girls and our boys.

The good news is that even your young children are likely very aware of some of the cultural movement and messages on sexual assault over the course of the past couple of years. The idea of consent must, of course, lie at the core of any discussions you engage in. And we need to prepare them for the reality that they will be hearing about sexual assault, and help them come up with a game plan should they ever fall into a situation that feels unsafe or compromising in any way. They also absolutely need to know that they can come to you, without question, in the wake of sexual assault.

Prevention here is critical. For those of us raising boys, we need to talk to them not just about consent, respect, and behavior, but what motivates men to these types of actions. I find that one of the most impactful methods for engaging in this talk with teenage boys is to solicit their thoughts on the matter. On the whole, they tend to offer keen insights into what leads to assault and how it can be prevented. Open, ongoing discussion can be successfully preventive and keeps that concept of consent in their mind's eye. Boys have shared with me that these talks with their parents are critical and so powerful. They can collectively create a cultural shift, changing the course of silent suffering for so many people, and the attitudes with which our young people consider each other's well-being, power dynamics, fear-based thinking, and toxic, externalized self-loathing.

I recently read about another dynamic among teenage boys that is reflected in my practice. Virtually to a boy, they *want* to be preventive here. That said, research suggests that teenage boys and young men know very little about the phenomenon, what defines sexual assault, what causes it, the impact on the victim, and how to prevent it. They know it's happening, of course, but they don't know what to do. I've worked with some teenage boys who are not sure they haven't committed sexual assault in the past, not sure where the lines are drawn.

Boys and young men are also poised, I find, to be open to new definitions of sexuality and masculinity. The idea of the "conquest" of women and racking up numbers of girls with whom they have hooked up ring hollow to teenage boys today. We need to support these notions in them. Individual and cultural change hangs in the balance, as does the elimination of unnecessary fear and anxiety in potential victims. Now is the time for these conversations, and I believe this is the generation that can achieve broad, lasting cultural change. We need to provide our children the information and tools to do so, especially for these confused young men.

In the wake of the #MeToo movement, and the use (and abuse, at times) of the phrase "toxic masculinity," I find many boys feel insecure, unsure, and ashamed. They are unclear about what masculinity looks like, as there is such a fine point put on what it should not be. But recently, the American Psychological Association began studying "positive masculinity," in part as an effort to guide young men toward a useful definition. Characteristics of positive masculinity include kindness, self-reliance, respect for women, courage, and a sense of humor. I believe that focusing on the positive elements of masculinity will help many young men find their bearings far more readily than solely hearing they are a blight on the culture, or predators whose dark, damaging impulses need to be reined in.

A few years back, I worked with a young man who had ostensibly come to therapy to discuss relationship issues with his current girlfriend. As his story unfolded, however, he disclosed the deep sense of shame he was carrying. Years earlier, he had sexually assaulted a girl, both of them intoxicated, at his fraternity house. His story reflects the layers of psychological underpinnings that such reprehensible actions tend to have, but it's an important cycle to understand. Nobody, including the victim, ever mentioned the assault to him. He recalls that, within the week, he felt a deep sense of relief that he might have gotten away with it. But the guilt and shame affiliated with his behavior that night have haunted him ever since.

As we talked about what drove this behavior, he confirmed what we so often hear about sexual assault—that it was not about sex. Instead, he affirmed, it was about power, and conquest, and proving himself a "man." Having been molested as a child himself, he thought perhaps this was a twisted way for him to subconsciously recoup his power and manhood. Upon deeper reflection, however, he realized his actions had more to do with his negative emotion toward himself than anything else. He discovered a sense of self-loathing he had disguised for years underneath swagger, power plays, and an overtly cocky attitude.

I think about this man, and the young woman who was his victim, frequently. I wonder whether open discussion in his family, decades ago, about sexual assault and power and the nature of masculinity, might have prevented the sexual assault that night at that frat house. I suppose that, in this case, we may never know.

We can engage in those conversations now with our children, and we need to.

Here's the good and bad news, all at once. Sexual assault is part of the national dialogue right now. Like so many issues you might prefer to put off for another year, your child is aware that sexual assault is in the news, and this does present an opportunity for discussion. Start gently, by asking questions about what they've heard, what they think about it, and how victims, and perpetrators, might feel. You can keep these conversations brief—a long sit-down might be overwhelming, especially for your younger children. But make sure you revisit the issue on occasion. There is an enormous opportunity, not only for prevention of sexual violence, but also for a deeper, richer respect for girls, women, and people in general.

This generation is poised to carry the mantle of a new way of thinking, a deeper sense of humanity and kindness and gentleness toward one another. They will play the roles. To my thinking, we just need to set the stage.

Suicide and Suicidal Ideation

The growth we've seen in recent years in the frequency of anxiety, depression, suicidal ideation, and hopelessness is not without consequence. The CDC reports that, with each passing year, we are losing more and more of our bright young people to suicide. You've probably been touched directly by one of these tragic losses, perhaps more than one. Rare is the middle school or high school in America today that goes a year or two without a loss to suicide. And you may notice clusters in your area, when the bodies stack up, leaving us all behind to question what we might have done to keep these children safe, drawing breath, thriving.

I am working with an eighteen-year-old girl, Julia. She has struggled with anxiety and depression for years but has never had a string of months in which she has been doing so well, effectively asymptomatic, until recently. Six weeks ago, however, she told me that the boyfriend of one of her closest friends took his own life. He shot himself while she sat, unaware of the depth of his despair, in the next room. Julia wrote me that evening, asking how she might best be supportive of her grieving friend. She handled this issue with the grace of a good friend who has been through enough that she was relatively unflappable, and her friend leaned on her heavily during her grieving period.

A month later, another friend of Julia's took her life. She reached out to this friend's parents and family, again comporting herself rather heroically, given the circumstances. Then one night not much later, Julia made an attempt on her own life. Reflecting back, she became overwhelmed by the "stench of death," as she described it, all around her: suicides, suicidal ideation, wakes, funerals, and seemingly unending grief.

I'd love to tell you that Julia's story is an aberration, that most kids are rarely if ever confronted with the notion of suicide. But this is simply not true. Suicide now affects nearly every high school and middle school, everywhere. Sadly and shockingly, some grade schools are now directly affected, and children as young as ten or eleven can be at risk. The idea of suicide is another frontier opening up to younger and younger children. Kids talk with one another, rather freely, about their thoughts of hopelessness and suicidal ideation, their vision of plans, and how people might react once they are gone. I have not worked with many teenagers in the past several years who have *not* engaged in this kind of discussion and thought.

Suicidal thoughts are becoming increasingly ordinary and pedestrian among young people.

So, as parents, we cannot avoid the discussion of suicide and suicidal ideation with our children. I have worked with more than one set of grieving parents who were wholly blindsided, unaware that suicide was even a thought in their child's mind. They would all argue that it is best to have an ongoing and open discussion with your child about suicide: whether they hear about it from peers, whether it has happened in any families they know, and, yes, whether they have ever considered it themselves.

I find that parents, quite understandably, can feel highly reluctant and queasy about that last mandate. I hear fears that children will be suggestible, somehow, if we introduce the idea of suicide to them, that we might be planting the seed of an idea that wasn't there before. Historically, there may have been a time when this was the case, and parents could protect children from that degree of hopelessness.

If so, that time is quite long gone. We *have* to talk to our kids about suicide and suicidal ideation, and we have to make ourselves fully available to them should they ever want to talk about either, regardless of our degree of discomfort with the topic. To provide you a modicum of comfort, I have engaged in discussions of suicide with virtually every teenager I have worked with, and not once did this result directly in a suicidal gesture. Instead, knowing she has someone to talk with, someone who is open, non-judgmental and not too afraid, is precisely what the teen suffering suicidal thoughts most needs.

Further, I find kids who tend toward depression and suicidal thoughts find enormous comfort in a safety plan.

Someone asked me recently why someone who wants to take their life would call their parent, or a therapist, or their counselor at school. I have learned that the answer is that no suicidal person truly wants to die. Rather, clients have described to me a "suicidal fog" in which all feels lost and hopeless. Providing them an option, a "call me without reservation," tends to allow for just enough hope to provide a beacon through the fog, one that can be truly lifesaving.

The bottom line is this: we are losing far too many young people to suicide—bright, talented, beautiful young people who cannot see past the moment. And we have culturally kept this issue under wraps, vaguely cloaked in shame, for far too long. If you have known someone who has taken their life, you will note that articles are typically not written on suicides for fear of "copycats" or suggestibility, and cause of death is omitted from obituaries. Meanwhile, suicide and suicidal ideation is somewhat misrepresented in the media, including some valiant attempts to address the issue and open dialogue, like *Thirteen Reasons Why*. In this Netflix series, the slights of a peer represent each of the thirteen reasons. Suicidality simply does not work this way.

The world our children are growing up in is a far harsher place than the one in which we came of age. Screens are not going away. The assault of overstimulation is only going to amplify, and to impact our children at ever-earlier ages. We therefore need to balance the harsh messages our children receive constantly with gentleness. They need to know, now more than ever, that they have a soft, available place to fall.

But on a micro level, within our own homes, we can talk, and we *must* talk. This is how we can do our part to lift the stigma, open the dialogue, and perhaps prevent the loss of another young life. Again, it is okay and imperative to be aware and to ask. Some questions to consider: Is your child quieter than she used to be? Is she down and sullen? Has her behavior and/or affect shifted dramatically? Is she spending more time alone?

Does she suddenly seem buoyant and relieved after a period of depression?

Any and all of these can be indications of suicidality, and there are many more precipitants, of course. That "suicide fog" can sweep over a child in the wake of a bad test score, or fear of a disciplinary issue, or aftermath of a sudden breakup. So, ask if she is okay. Be receptive to the answer, especially if it is a no.

It bears repeating here that I have noticed a dramatic boost in quasi-suicidal thinking, that idea that "I am not going to do anything to hurt myself, but I don't care if I wake up tomorrow, either" thinking. I want this potentiality to be on your mind when talking to your child, to remind you that it may be lurking somewhere in her mind. We want to be just as open to addressing this type of thinking with our children. "Does this have to do with the way you feel about yourself? The world? The future?"

A Course of Action if Your Teen Is Suicidal

Given that these can be issues of immediate health and safety, I want you to have a clear course of action if you feel your child's concerns may be beyond your expertise. Should your child express that she is overtly suicidal in the moment that you ask, the only plan, immediately, is to call 911. This will ensure her safety, right away. And you will have professionals available to guide you through the next steps.

If your child expresses some degree of suicidal ideation, but she does not have a plan and clearly is no immediate threat to herself, please seek a qualified therapist for her right away. That professional would be a psychologist or licensed clinical social worker, with specific experience working with young people who have experienced these feelings. It's a mighty parent, to my thinking, that has the presence of mind to use all of the tools at her disposal to help her child regain a sense of safety and well-being.

Part Three

FILLING YOUR TOOLBOX

The Vibe in Your Home

In early sessions with teenagers, I usually ask about the overall vibe they experience at home: "As you cross the threshold, do you find home to be more of a refuge or more of a stressor?"

Too often, the answer is the latter. Home feels tense and stressful for a lot of teenagers. The reasons vary quite a bit. Some kids tell me their parents don't get along. Others tell me it's too noisy at home, and others too quiet. Some feel judged whenever they are home. Some feel they are under constant watch, and some feel invisible.

The broad point is, kids are very aware of the vibe of their home, and the majority describe to me a vibe that is, at the least, undesirable.

It is so very important, therefore, to create a vibe in your home that is warm, comfortable, and reasonably happy. Remember, there is emotional traffic swirling around your children constantly. We want home to be a place where they can put their minds in Park, hear themselves think, and allow themselves to breathe. If you and home are a part of the onslaught, the traffic, they will never feel free of it. Eventually, like anyone, your child will burn out. And burnout usually looks awfully symptomatic: depression, anxiety, ADHD, and so on.

So, make home a sanctuary. Consider your home in a sensory way, how the spaces feel and how you feel in them. Set your home up so that your kids do not spend the lion's share of their time isolated, up in a bedroom, door closed, identity traffic blaring. Make the common areas of your home welcome spaces to work and connect and eat and laugh. Help your children organically achieve a sense of balance by providing that space and that vibe.

Consider other elements of the vibe at home as well. Is there a television on all the time, adding to the traffic? Turn that thing off unless someone is watching something specific. Are we arguing more than connecting? Find a tone and tenor that feels better. Is it so quiet that it feels lifeless? Take charge of infusing your space with some light and laughter.

You do not need to be an expert in feng shui to make these changes. In fact, in most of this fine-tuning of the home vibe, you can use your own senses as a guide for your child's, as I find this is one area in which parents and kids tend to agree. If you are uncomfortable in your home, your child likely is as well.

My wife and I stumbled upon a fortunate reality when we bought our house. I was recently out of graduate school, and we could only afford a small home in the neighborhood we wanted. As my son approached the teen years, he naturally did his homework at the dining room table. After all, the bedrooms were small, and he wanted some space. We also decided early on not to place computers, TVs, or phones in the bedrooms at home. So we were typically found in the common areas of our home. If George wanted privacy, he could always go to the basement or his bedroom. But his default was, by and large, to remain in the common area. This turned out to be so fortuitous, as either Julie or I was right there if George needed help with something or wanted to talk something through. Otherwise, we all went about our business in the same space.

Every once in a while, virtually every night, the silence
would be broken by a discussion or a joke or maybe a bizarre
impromptu sing-along (seriously, we would do that. We still
do). These disruptions served to alleviate tension, and built up
the Emotional Bank Account. I honestly think our use of space
plays a role in how close the three of us are to this day, with
George approaching his mid-twenties.

Now again, I would love to say that it was my psychological
brilliance that drove this fortuitous situation. But it was not.
We stumbled upon this vibe quite by accident. But I think you
should consider borrowing from it. My clientele spend far
too much time alone in their rooms, doors closed, away from
family. I suspect a lot of the difficulties we are discussing here
could be mitigated by using space in the home differently and
spending more time together than apart.

I cannot stress enough how important this issue is to the well-
being of your children. And, too often, it is a hidden issue,
rearing its head in other ways. An uncomfortable home may
manifest in a negative behavior or stressed affect on the part of
your child. Don't let it come to that. Allow a quick gut check.
You probably know already a change or two you can make to set
the tone you want, for yourself and your child, at home.

As you can read here, there are countless issues drawing down
the well-being of your child, be it smartphones, the pressure to
do well and fit into the proper definition of success, academic
issues, social issues, or overall issues of self-esteem. As best
we can, we want to inoculate our children from these cultural
difficulties. Creating a home atmosphere with a relatively
happy, comfortable vibe is one of those rare areas in which we

parents can exert an enormous amount of agency. I strongly encourage you to attend to it and create that positive, accepting, loving, gentle vibe.

Awe and Wonder

During a recent early December coaching session, a mom was lamenting the dearth of awe and wonder at the time of year for her young sons. She went on to say that she grew up in awe of Christmas, Santa Claus (or the *idea* of Santa, the magic of Santa), the music and other trappings, and the excitement of Christmas morning. Her sons, now both in their early teens, made lists and helped decorate, but the process was relatively joyless. Where was the awe and wonder? She thought she might have another year or two of it, especially with her younger son. And as she said sadly, "Nobody told me this part was going to be over so soon."

As the session went on, we both realized that awe and wonder were two elements sorely lacking from the lives of children overall these days. Because of all the stimuli they are exposed to, kids become discerning pragmatists at ever-earlier ages. They train themselves to peek behind the veil of anything they see, and put it to the sniff test of their reality. Because we have culturally created the circumstances by which they are now skeptics from an early age, awe and wonder are the prices that our children pay and, secondarily, that we pay ourselves.

We are consciously aware that we miss our children being innocent, unquestioning, and *little* in every sense.

I like working with this mom. She is smart, kind, thoughtful, and available. She was not willing to settle for the idea that, simply because we have entered a new age, our kids will just have to live a life free of the joys that the senses of awe and wonder bring.

So, by the next session, she had arrived at a solution, or a partial solution, at the least. She decided that, because of iPhones, iPads, computers, TVs, and other screens, there was likely no *thing* that was going to bring awe and wonder back into the lives of our kids. But she remembered a recent European vacation she had taken with her family. Walking through unfamiliar museums and plazas, hearing different languages, and being fully immersed in a different culture, she clearly remembers seeing awe and wonder returning to the faces of her children. She reminded me that travel and a new setting brought this out in my son too. Hell, travel brought the awe and wonder out in me.

The conclusion we came to that day, and that I adhere to up to this moment, is that she was right. No thing was going to bring awe and wonder back to our kids once they had breached that developmental moment. Physical stuff was no longer the answer. Instead, awe and wonder could only be gained through experience: travel, a Broadway play, live music, the first view of mountains when the fog clears, the exhilaration of the ocean on a sunny day.

So, if you lament the missing awe and wonder in your child's eyes, and you fear that once it's gone, it's gone, I strongly encourage you to avoid Amazon and the mall, and seek out experiences for that look in your child's eyes. Now, I fully understand that a European vacation may not be in the budget for you, but I know that some awe-inspiring experience is. Play some music together. Go camping for a couple of nights. Get your child out of context, away from her phone and other devices, and watch her slowly light up.

Inspiring Awe and Wonder

You may read this chapter and wonder how to inspire kids in this day when it is ever so difficult to impress them and, sometimes, to even gain their undivided attention. Following are a few adventures I have found catch kids in awe, often despite themselves.

First, if you have the means, consider enriching family vacations. Head to DC instead of Orlando, and go for the cultural experience. Your kids will surprise you with the degree to which they appreciate this shift. Visit the national parks, and actually stop when you see something interesting. Take a hike off the beaten path. Visit any city, anywhere on the planet, and seek out the life of the locals instead of the life of the tourists (Rick Steves's travel guides will help here).

I recently surveyed my son, some of his friends, and a number of young clients on what inspired awe and wonder in them. The responses included live music, the outdoors, sporting events (live: in the arena, in the stands, at the pool, and so on), the ocean, talk about philosophy, and exposure to political rallies in person.

Kids are naturally drawn to experiences more than material things and often describe them as transcendent and life-altering. This is what they remember and can be the basis for a lot of their passions later in their lives. This is a great parenting guide for fostering awe and wonder in your kids.

> Please do not underestimate the importance of this in their development as inspired, excited, life-filled adults.
>
> Awe and wonder can create a critical counterpoint to the anxiety that occupies the remainder of their lives.

Doing Away with the Sedentary Days

Certain elements of childhood are quickly falling away with the onslaught of so much stimuli impacting our children's minds. The concept of *play*, a critical component of development, of sharing and cooperation and stress management, is primary among them. You will notice that kids do not play much today the way you likely played when you were a child: pretend games, made-up scenarios, running and jumping with abandon like their young bodies are organically drawn to do.

Corresponding to the lack of play is a tendency to be indoors more frequently than any generation before them. This becomes apparent as we watch our kids brighten and energize and rediscover their childhood when they are out. Just attend to your kids' shift in energy when you are out on vacation, or sightseeing, or letterboxing (a favorite outdoor pastime for the Duffy family for the better part of two decades—check out letterboxing.org to learn more). Watch them when they step onto the field or court, jump into the pool, run down the beach toward the ocean. Watch them take in the awe of nature organically. With all the weight of the anxieties described here bearing down on them, they need so much more of that in their lives.

So, I find that a lot of the pent-up, anxious energy kids display is, at least in part, an artifact of an increasingly sedentary young life. There are countless issues that could be resolved if we could reinstall the concepts of play, and sport, and exercise into our children's lives.

The clarion call here for parents could not be clearer. Because the culture surrounding them will provide those opportunities only rarely, we need to provide those opportunities to our children frequently. Too often, I find kids default to the basement couch or their bed upstairs. This is not in their authentic nature, and their minds and their bodies become restless, anxious, out of sorts, and out of balance. I find nature, and sports in particular, to be tremendous regulators in this regard.

I do not encourage parents to play the "Yes, you have to, simply because I said so" parent card very often. Not for chores or homework or cleaning the room. But for this, for forcing activity, I strongly encourage you to play the parent card. Kids modulate and regulate themselves best emotionally, academically, physically, and intellectually when they tire out their bodies over the course of the day. I know this, as I see it in my clients year after year. For many kids, they perform better academically when super busy and "in-season" in their sport than when they have hours of unstructured, under-scheduled time in their days. They plan better. They sleep better. And they regulate better.

Participation in sports also limits the time your kids spend looking down, vaping, moping, and worrying.

There simply is no downside.

Yeah, It Takes a Village

There are times when it is critically important to trust your child with another adult, one with her best interests in mind: teachers, coaches, directors, and other mentors, to name a few. Spending time with these adults can build the competence and resilience our children need for future success.

We need to remember the potential positive effects that strong relationships with extended family, for example, can have on our children. The guidance and input of grandparents, aunts, and uncles can prove beyond invaluable.

As a clinician, I love when aunts and uncles are deeply involved in the lives of kids. The teenagers I work with turn to these family members when they have issues Mom and Dad might not be altogether comfortable with. In some instances, the sex talk or the drug talk can be as effective, if not more so, when it comes from an aunt and/or an uncle (in addition, of course, to the talks you offer your children). These extended family members sometimes feel more comfortable than parents in discussing certain topics, and can be more direct at times, or offer a relieving air of levity.

I worked with a teenage girl recently who posted something inappropriate on Instagram. She had a pre-existing agreement with her aunt that they would follow each other. Upon seeing the inappropriate post, her aunt playfully texted, "You have ten minutes to pull the post before I reach out to Mom or Dad!"

Problem quickly solved. Message immediately received.

I also work with a young boy who has been experiencing difficulty getting along with his father. While they are working things through, the boy's uncle, Dad's brother, is stepping in. He is helping with homework, offering advice on social issues, and advising on how to patch things up with his dad.

On the whole, I find that kids with strong relationships with aunts and uncles thrive. They value them deeply and feel cared for by a number of loving adults. In these times, our children may need more than one soft place to fall. Aunts and uncles are perfect additions to your child's support system.

They are perfect additions, but there are other adults out there ready to help as well.

I recently worked with a mom whose seventeen-year-old son William and his friends had recently started drinking. After one long night, Carter, a good friend of William's, drank too much. He stumbled out of the party, and police found him passed out in the street. Now, this is not the first time I've heard a story like this in session, nor will it be the last. But the way Carter's parents handled it was quite unusual.

In my experience, most of us as parents are so mortified in situations like this that we go into a sort of hiding. We do not communicate with the parents in the area, and we certainly do not discuss what happened. At best, some of us would make our kids reach out to any inconvenienced parents to apologize.

Carter's parents decided that, in order to really address the drinking issue going on between him and his friends, they would be forthcoming. They sent an email to the parents of all the kids involved and told their story: the fear, the ER visit, the post-mortem the next day, all of it. I love this approach. The more we tell our stories, the more we lift unnecessary, anxiety-provoking taboos, and provide other people with permission to tell their own. If this was all they had accomplished, that would have been tremendous, in my opinion.

But it went further than that. They discussed how they might work together as a community to ensure their kids were, at the very least, safe. A couple of parents reached out to them immediately with both support and ideas. They are working out ways to manage this together. I just love this idea, and the nature of this gesture. Nobody was shamed or blamed. And the goal is the safety of the teenagers going forward. A community can play a hefty role in helping in this regard.

Parenting is a big job these days and, as you can tell from simply reading this book, it's growing bigger by the year. It is not something we can accomplish alone, not anymore. These days, it really does take a village, a community, to raise a child.

Our communal role, by the way, does not only involve health, safety, and admonishing a child. It also means smiling at a child whose head is hanging low, walking down the street. It's letting your nieces and nephews know you are always there for them if they need someone to talk with and are reluctant to engage

Mom or Dad. It means checking in with your child's friends to ask how they're doing these days. If you are wondering whether to address a child, consider the better story, the next right thing to do, for just a moment. That goes for any parent, any adult, who might be reading here, and any teenagers who are reading as well.

Finally, we parents are not always going to be the most effective at guiding our child toward her greatness. We may be overly harsh, personally invested, or soft. My wife Julie and I, for instance, are softies. We never really wanted George to experience much discomfort, physically, emotionally, or otherwise.

When George was a high school freshman, he told us he wanted to join the swim team. I thought this was a bad idea. Swimmers are a unique brand. They work so hard. They get up early and push themselves to the physical brink. Then they do the same thing after school. For hours. I didn't think George would like it.

On Day One, we parents had a meeting with the coach. He encouraged us to trust him with our son. He told us George would be tired, sore, and cranky at times throughout the season. And he encouraged us to trust him. So, for some reason, we did. And George rose to the occasion. He was that guy who got up at the crack of dawn to get to work. He worked in the pool after school. He worked hard for four years. He pressed and competed, lost and won, and made some of his best friends for life.

But before any of that happened, we had to trust the coach. And Coach Scott Walker knew he could build the self-worth of sixty-five boys by pushing them, by showing them what they were capable of doing. Julie and I, we were never going to be able to do this for George.

Somewhere in your child's life waits a Coach Walker. Part of being a strong and mighty parent is to guide your child toward that adult, that adult who is going to hold a mirror up so that she can fully see herself, strong and capable and competent and resilient. To my thinking, this is among the most important things we can do as parents: outsource the parts of raising an adult that we cannot do, to those who can.

One final note here: Some of your kids will need a therapist during their adolescent journey. Please do not underestimate the power and potency of that relationship as one your child can lean on as well, one that will help carry her through emotionally.

Getting her the help she needs, when she needs it. That's mighty parenting too.

Can We Skip This Part?

A very thoughtful, caring mother of an eight-year-old boy was musing recently about whether there was an alternative to all the tumult described here, whether she might be able to avoid all of this stimuli, anxiety, and identity traffic for her son. After all, she rightly noted, he is smart, curious, and adaptable, and he connects well with adults. He is a talented student, musician, and athlete. Why not skip some of the inevitable social pitfalls, the idea that depression is either cool or necessary, the feeling that he needs to rely on drugs to function sufficiently in the world? Why not control the atmosphere, home-school him, get him involved in a sport and some private music lessons? Doesn't he then emerge from these teen years relatively unscathed?

The party line on this approach is, of course, a hard no. The primary argument involves socialization: How will he ever learn to connect with people with differing thoughts, interests, proclivities? How will he learn to share and cooperate? These are, after all, among the building blocks for success, right?

Well, this mom is savvy and smart. She thinks outside the box, so this argument was not so easily won.

"We can teach him cooperation. He won't be living in isolation after all. He has to cooperate and negotiate relationships with his dad and me, with his siblings. And what are kids really learning from one another that's productive and adaptive? By keeping him in school and 'playing by the rules of convention,' as it were, aren't we exposing him to every fate and pitfall exposed in every chapter of your book? We can mitigate that. As parents, isn't that a pretty good mandate?" I couldn't entirely disagree with her. After all, her son is really bright. He tests well. He will get into a good school, yes? I could not disagree with that entirely either.

She is convinced a protective bubble will serve her son best. And I get it.

So, after a lot of thought, here's why I think it's important, despite all of the negatives described in this book, that we play the game, send our kids to school, expose them to it all. As indicated, I have found that there are two fundamental goals to parenting. If we can guide our children toward the development of these two characteristics, they will be able to manage any storm presented to them in their adult lives—and we all know, there *will* be storms.

Those goals have not changed in decades. The goals of parenting are competence and resilience. Consider for a moment the utility of these two qualities. If your teenager is competent when she heads off to college or her next adventure in life, the confidence, self-worth, and self-esteem that accompany that quality will carry her through the tasks of her life. She will know she is capable of her work. She will trust her instincts in relationships. She will manage money well. The benefits are virtually impossible to quantify, but they are plentiful.

The resilient teenager knows she can handle things when they become difficult. She will have faced challenges, many of them described in this book, and she will have overcome them. Sometimes, the road will be rocky, but if she can reflect back and see that she has made it through some trying circumstances, that will only serve to bolster her confidence that she can do so again regardless of the difficulties presented to her in the future.

So, the parenting protocol this mom describes may bolster the former, competence. If she shields him from the anxieties, vices, and other challenges of adolescence, her child will have been exposed to academic, social, and musical challenges. He may well gain admission into an elite collegiate institution. He will be capable and competent.

My concern for him would be the latter, resilience. Will he have been exposed to enough difficulty, enough of the real world, the world the vast majority of his age group has navigated, to really know that he is resilient? Or will he be blindsided as a young adult, struck by the harshness of the world once he is released from the bubble of safety? Will he be one of those college freshmen or sophomores, perhaps even a recent college grad, scrambling home unable to regulate himself within that harsh world, wholly new to him?

I sincerely believe that the better story for nearly any child is to go through it, instead of navigating safely around it. Here, I think the concept of safety itself is a bit of a misnomer. We can keep our kids safe from the real world for a time, I suppose, following something like the methodology this mom is proposing. But in the end, we want our kids to be exposed to the world. That's where all the challenges are, to be sure. But it's also where the joy resides, and the fullest life, challenges and all.

Living a life filled with rich experiences might be perilous, but it also provides our kids with a sense of belonging, connection, and joy. This is the good stuff. This is a beautiful time in life. These years are where we make lifelong friendships, fall in love, carry each other, meet new teachers and mentors, find our way. This is not something you want your kids to skip. This is the most beautiful part of life.

I am aware I present a somewhat dystopian picture of the prolonged teenage universe here. I do that in large part to raise your level of awareness, so that you are as equipped as you can be to parent effectively through the storms. But every child experiences joys and connections and victories and laughter. Developmentally, it is important to experience it all, to recognize the emotional nuances of every situation and that there will be defeats and sadness, anxiety and loneliness, along the way. There will also be laughter, and joy, and abject happiness.

In response to this mom, I suggest that we are doing our children a wild disservice by protecting them from any of it. Of course, we need to remain available throughout, as allies, guides, and consultants. But our children need to feel as if they have done it, been through it, navigated it, as the primary contractors on their personal paths through these times. This progression is imperative. It provides them a sense both of who they are and of what they can handle.

And they need to know that they are competent and resilient throughout. To my thinking, simply trusting that they can navigate the tangle socially, academically, emotionally, and otherwise provides the show of confidence that can carry them successfully, not just through adolescence, but throughout their adulthood. It is among the most critical tasks of parenting.

Music

In some form, I suspect this section could have been written a generation ago, and a generation before that. Most of us, I find, are not interested in, perhaps are even appalled at, the music our kids choose to listen to. We find rap and hip-hop particularly and unnecessarily vulgar and, in the words of one mom, an assault on the ears. I think we all feel as if we have become frighteningly like our parents in this respect, prudes who just don't get it.

You may be offended by the swearing in rap music, and by the fact that your child is willing to listen to it, loudly, in the car, with you. You may be put off by the misogyny, the hedonism, the drug and alcohol use and abuse so frequently depicted, the lack of any morality. In retrospect, I'll bet this sounds like one or both of your own parents talking to you about your music decades ago.

But let's remember for a moment what music does for us, especially through the teen years. Your teenager does not listen to a particular type of music to test your parenting acumen, or to get under your skin. Her music has precious little to do with you. Rather, she listens because she enjoys her music. In some ways, just like your teenage soundtrack spoke to you a generation ago (and, if you're like me, probably still does), her music brings color and meaning and understanding to her life.

My strong bias in terms of approach to music: listen with her. Place your biases on hold, and really get into this. It can prove priceless, for your teenager and for your relationship. I guarantee that you will leave this session having enjoyed yourself more than you would have thought possible and having connected with your child in a new and most important way.

So, sit down while she's listening, and play her music with her. I have done this with countless teenagers over the years, buzzing through playlists on our phones, sometimes curious as to whether my suite-mates, or parents leafing through magazines in my waiting room, wonder whether any work is getting done in my office at all. Regardless, you will find any time listening to her music heartening, for your child is not likely listening for the misogyny and hedonism. She is listening because the music touches her emotionally somehow. In all likelihood, you will learn that her music, whatever form it may take, speaks to her, and makes her feel understood and less alone. It may be noise to you, but it probably rings more like hope to her. So, listen with her. She will think you're cool for doing so, especially if you go into this with an open mind. And, you will understand her far better than you would imagine. This should be fun, by the way, if you're truly open and available to it, and your biases are put aside.

And if you're like me, you just might find that you enjoy and appreciate the music itself as well. You may find in yourself a deeper understanding of her entire generation too. For she will show you what is not apparent on the surface, a vibe or feeling a certain beat brings to her or the depth and meaning of a lyric you thought you understood. Get into it. Dig it. It'll be worth it.

Earbuds and Homework

After all the discussion in my office on this topic over the decades, I will never buy the argument, put forth by many of the teens I have worked with, that they complete their homework more effectively when listening to music. On the whole, I just don't believe that's true, and my point of view is supported by research. So, my strong bias would be that the earbuds or AirPods are *out* when your teenager is doing homework. During homework breaks, or once it's completed, sure. But when trying to write a paper, learn a language, or complete a complex math problem, the less outside stimulation, the better.

That said, I have been persuaded of the occasional exception here. Some kids have convinced me that they can listen to classical music, ambient or electronic music, or a wordless Spotify playlist, and that the sound helps them to relax and focus. I'll buy that. Rap or metal, not so much.

Sleep, from P.M. to A.M.

Sleep is the oft-neglected component of parenting effectively, the area I find parents are most likely to throw up their arms in surrender about. We all know sleep is important, but, in many households, it feels like a battle either lost or not worth fighting.

If you count yourself among the parents who have given up the sleep-related battle, allow me to encourage you here to reengage. Silently, sleep issues have become epidemic among teenagers over the past several years. I'm well aware that these problems among young people go back generations, but they are far, far worse today, and absolutely bear mentioning and resolving here.

Lack of a solid night's sleep can cause far more than fatigue in your child. Lack of sleep can deplete resilience over the course of a day. It can mirror, symptom by symptom, every single element of attention issues and ADHD. I have worked with literally hundreds of children medicated for this issue that I fear may just be overly fatigued and wholly unaware. I very often discover that what looks like a learning, or perhaps even a neurological, issue is actually just a brain running on fumes by the end of the school day, deprived of the deep rest it needs to function and develop properly.

Relevant recent research also suggests, with alarming clarity, that a great deal of the anxiety and depression we see in teens would resolve quickly if they slept better. In fact, one study found that sleep was the primary variable that produced the most change in both depression and anxiety.

In my experience, there are two primary factors in sleep issues for today's teenagers. One is the lack of a consistent bedtime and bedtime ritual. I strongly suggest a hard reset here if your child is not sleeping enough. Keep in mind the guideline, supported by many sleep doctors, that your child likely needs eight to ten hours of uninterrupted sleep per night. It's also important to note that the notion many of us hold that we can somehow make up for lost sleep on the weekend is pure fallacy.

Now, being pragmatic for a moment, I do not know many teenagers who get this much sleep, not even close. But my bias is to push for eight hours, and making that happen requires routine. And so many kids either have no routine whatsoever for bedtime, or wholly ineffective routines. First, I cannot state enough how counterproductive a screen can be in your child's room, particularly at night. The vast majority of teens I know, for instance, keep their phone at the bedside, ostensibly to use as an alarm clock. And there is truth here, as most kids do use them for specifically this purpose. But let's be honest. There are an awful lot more stimuli available than an alarm on that device, stimuli that may keep your child awake and engaged, silently, long into the night. Nothing robs today's teenagers of precious REM sleep more efficiently, silently, and effectively than a smartphone. Nothing. The illuminated screen is super stimulating, rousing the brain rather than resting it. Every notification does the same. And alarming recent research suggests that just knowing the phone is activated, even if on sleep mode, is stimulating enough to keep a child awake for hours. This happens in adults as well, by the way.

Kids routinely tell me that they will check their phone impulsively when falling asleep or even when they wake up in the middle of the night. And don't forget, most of the activity your child engages in on their smartphone is entirely silent. If the phone is in her room, and she is texting a friend, reviewing her feeds on Instagram, completing streaks on Snapchat, or watching a YouTube video or even pornography, you are unlikely to be made aware of it.

So, here's a need for a hard reset in your home, preferably today. Phones and tablets either never go upstairs or to bedrooms or, at the very least, they are never allowed in bedrooms overnight. When I can get a family to practice this simple, but not easy, shift, sleep issues often fall away readily. In order to get the rule to stick, by the way, I find that you parents will need to follow it yourself. It's a lot to ask, I know, especially if your family, like most, is deeply ingrained in the habit of looking at your phone in the moments before you close your eyes, but the dividends are immeasurable.

So, head over to Target and buy some alarm clocks.

That may seem to be the tough part, but there's a deeper mandate here for a routine to become fixed. Your child cannot be the only one sticking to it. You need to practice what you preach here and model good nighttime routines, going to bed at a consistent time, and finding and sticking to an effective method for your own wind-down to the day.

The other critical issue when it comes to sleep, by the way, is a consistent wake-up time, especially during the week throughout the school year. Those first moments of the mornings are so crucial in setting a tone for the day, and far too many families begin their day, nearly every day, with an argument about getting out of bed. I suspect many of you are nodding vigorously as you read this paragraph. As it turns out, this is a very difficult problem to eradicate once established. In my experience, the most effective way to do this is to make your teenager responsible for getting herself up and out of bed. The benefit here is twofold. First, you eliminate the morning arguments that set that negative tone for the day for your entire family. Second, your teenager gains some of that internal sense of competence and resilience.

The tough part is getting started, especially if you are already in the habit of waking her up yourself, over and over again, with conflict inevitably on the back end. I find that this, like so many parenting issues, requires a hard reset. This means setting an entirely different set of wake-up parameters: "You are now 100 percent responsible for getting yourself up." Releasing this responsibility is wildly difficult for many parents to do. In fact, some of my client parents feel it's negligent, at least to an extent, not to take on the wake-up chore for their child. Let me assure you, however, that it is not.

Still, this technique may not be "successful" right away. Herein lies one of those instances in which your child may need to feel the pinch of a natural consequence in order to recognize the gravity of the responsibility, that the weight of it lies on her shoulders and, most importantly, that she has agency over the issue from this day forward. So, if you sit down for a brief meeting and agree that the responsibility for waking up shifts to her, I strongly urge you to live by the rule yourself. Should she sleep late one day, shutting off her alarm and going back to sleep, then she's late.

If she misses half a day of school once, she misses half a day of school. The lesson learned in holding personal responsibility and taking ownership of one's life is far more potent and impactful than anything happening in a few hours of missed class. And better that it happen now, under the security of your own roof, than years from now, when she is away at college and continuing a bad habit that can have true long-term negative consequences on her life.

Remember, if all goes well, your child will not always live under your roof. Sometime soon, she will need to be responsible for herself in nearly every way. If she does not, for instance, get accustomed to getting the day started on her own now, imagine how difficult it will be for her to initiate that habit while first away at college, or in her own apartment. Better to rest now, and build a better, far more adaptive set of habits.

I find that poor sleep can contribute to so many emotional, physical, and behavioral difficulties that I would have been entirely remiss to exclude this discussion. Attend to sleep. It may save you and your child a world of problems.

Oh, and one brief, final note on this issue, based on my clinical experience. Teenagers rarely, if ever, need naps. I find them disruptive to the process, and, in the hours when teens are drawn to napping, I would far, far prefer they be on a field, a court, a stage, a pool, or in a concert hall. In my experience, napping as a habit is depressing, for all of us. Teenagers who nap, I find, tend to sleep more poorly at night, become dysregulated in the mornings, and often miss either parts of school days, or entire days. They also present as sluggish or lethargic, not energized and excited about life. As I reflect on decades with teenagers in my practice, I can think of precious few exceptions to this rule.

The Value of Money

In a recent session, a father was addressing me about his son, sitting next to him on the couch. "Also," he screamed, "he has no appreciation for hard-earned money! He just spends it all willy-nilly, without a thought. I don't think he understands the value of money!" Then from the other side of the couch, calmly:

"No, I don't. Where would I have learned that?"

I had been in this precise space before with other families, so I intervened. This young man was right. Kids today, honestly, have precious little opportunity to truly learn, and really comprehend, the value of a dollar. Consider for a moment your wallet when you were a teenager. Speaking for myself, I carried only cash. When I paid for something, I gained a quick visual of what I had spent and what remained. When I was working, my paycheck delineated what I had gained and what I was losing via various taxes. The reality was harsh, but undeniable.

Now, money may seem an odd topic to write about here, but it causes a tremendous degree of strife in families and truly is a significant blind spot for many kids.

Think about how rarely today a child handles actual currency. Hardly ever. And kids who work can gain a fresher perspective on value, but even that money tends to be virtual, direct-deposited into an account. Apps like Venmo make money feel more virtual, and some kids receive payment for anything from sneakers to chores via Square, a tiny device that swipes credit cards directly from a phone or iPad. Clever, but virtual.

In another recent session, a father arrived with a financial presentation which I'm certain he felt was going to reap dividends with in educating his teenage daughter. He brought in a hard copy of his paycheck, along with an extensive, detailed spreadsheet delineating all the areas where his hard-earned money went. The bottom line was the paltry sum he was able to save every two weeks.

It was, frankly, a damn good idea.

But he delivered his message in the form of not only a lecture, but an angry, shaming lecture. He pointed out, angrily, how much she spent every two weeks on unnecessary items: clothes, movies, Starbucks, meals out, and so on. Again, I thought the idea was sound, but the delivery fell flat. In fact, it was counterproductive, as Dad was considering the *literal* bank account, while ignoring entirely the Emotional Bank Account that might have allowed his message to be heard.

Contrast that with the father I worked with a couple of years ago, sitting across from his son, a soon-to-be college sophomore. His son had underperformed in freshman year, due to some of the self-regulation issues discussed above. In session, he made a real-time plea to his father to allow him to return, on probation, for another semester.

His father, who had handled this issue with abundant grace and support to date, said to him, "I love you, and I promise you I will support any reasonable endeavor you ever embark upon. But we are talking about twenty-five thousand dollars. Twenty-five thousand. And you have proven yourself to be a good man and a good son. But right now, you are a very poor investment."

He explained further, briefly, before his son fully agreed. He recognized that twenty-five thousand dollars was an awful lot of money, that his father had, effectively, gambled on him twice in the past year and lost that investment, and he understood why he wasn't willing to do so again. Not now at least.

The difference here lies, as you likely know by now, in the judicious use of the Emotional Bank Account.

One final note on money and finances. It may seem obvious, but I do find that once kids get a job and are responsible for their own spending, or at the very least some percentage of their own spending, they quickly learn the value of a dollar and become frugal themselves. They really do.

Teaching the Value of Money, Sans Lecture

I suggest parents bring their children with them when they shop, show them comparisons in a grocery store, or Target, or a car lot, between one purchase and another. Bring them into the discussion this way.

I also really like the idea, quite honestly, of "Bring your child to work" days. Though for reasons of confidentiality, this is something I will never be able to do myself, I have worked with many kids who disclose that days like that were revelatory to them. They had no previous idea of either the nature or the difficulty of their parents' days, and spending that time with them produced a degree of understanding and empathy. It also provided them context regarding the value of money. Such a worthwhile endeavor, and I wish this were provided by organizations not just for young children, but for teenagers as well. I think teens are better positioned to truly gain from the lessons learned over the course of such a day, no kidding.

What You Can Do Now

I can imagine getting this far in the book, having the veil lifted on the enormous, quantum shift in the teenage years, and being a bit overwhelmed. You may think, "Okay, I get it. What exactly can I do to help my child manage it all with more ease and grace, and less stress and anxiety?"

The following are some steps you can begin to take immediately to cultivate exactly that result.

First, you can work on being more available, connecting with your child free of fear, judgment, and ego. Remember, your child is highly empathic, and even senses your pain and discomfort. If you can table that, even for moments at a time, you will be providing your child with the non-judgmental ear she needs. The truth is, she rarely needs you to solve anything for her. And she does not benefit one bit from your lectures. But your open and available ear will mean the world to her and protect the space she needs to make sense of all the confusion she carries. This you can do starting today, right now. If you have not read my first book, I strongly suggest you pick it up to guide you through this process.

You can also venture deeper into your child's world right now: not as a spy, but as an ally. You can ask about what you don't understand, about social media, about depression, about anxiety, about the dynamics in her class. Allow yourself to be curious. Again, I find that kids like to teach and can be very sound, insightful instructors. I've asked some kids why they haven't walked their parents through some of these elements of their lives. Typically, the answer is, "They never asked."

So, ask.

One brief note here: do not expect your child to open up the first time you ask. If this process is new to her, she may just offer sound bites, moments of insight. Work with those. Slowly work your way toward gaining more insight into her life. It will likely not all come at once. And that's okay. Just knowing that you're interested will help her feel less alone in the muck of it all.

You also need to be willing to hear *everything* she has to say about her life. You cannot set a cutoff point based on your degree of upset or anxiety or your lack of desire to listen. It's usually right at the point of discomfort that the most important information she has to share may arise. You do not want to deprive her of sharing any of that. Remember that, in a way, your child is fighting for her life here. And these conversations may just be the life preserver she needs. Keep that in mind, and you will recognize fairly easily that her needs supersede any anxiety you may be experiencing in listening.

You can also play the parent card, judiciously, right now. If your child is wholly disengaged, body and mind accumulating anxiety in her room or on the couch, screen situated in hand, then play the parent card. That is, mandate that she engage in something: a sport, a club, a play, music lessons, a job at the grocery store, something. She doesn't need to love it or even like it. But the parent card suggests she has to do it. By playing the card, you are allowing a seed of competence and resilience to be planted. You are getting that body in motion. It may shift direction with time and experience and likely will. But sometimes, your child is lost enough that the parent card is necessary to kickstart the process.

If you feel disconnected from your child, you can also execute the hard reset, right now. That is, you can recognize, out loud, that your relationship as it stands is not working and that you intend to do your part in changing the dynamic between you, right now. This circumvents the need to go back in time and talk about who's to blame and why things went south and so on. Rather, the hard reset is a recognition of the way things are, a radical acceptance of the reality, and a plan to move forward.

This will change the conversation. That can be as simple as, "From this moment on, I intend to be your ally. I will listen to you, and I expect you will show me that same respect. I love you, and I want only the best for you, today and always. I want to understand, and I accept you and love you no matter what. So, let's start now to work together to make that happen."

I'll remind you that every parent, and every child, wants the same thing. We all want that connection. This is a great new start. It may be a bit bumpy going forward, but that intention will change the dynamic with time. It's a sure win-win. And your child *needs* you as a partner through this morass.

With any of these recommendations, if you feel as if you cannot get yourself there emotionally or pragmatically, if you feel that connection is too frayed or your situation is simply too difficult to navigate, get in to talk to a professional right away, a qualified therapist or parent coach. And if you see even a remote need, find a professional therapist for your child as well.

Perhaps the most important thing you can do as a parent is emotional housekeeping. Make sure you are emotionally aware and secure yourself, that you are protecting ample time for self-care, and that unresolved issues in your life aren't bleeding into your relationship with your child. This is good modeling of emotional well-being, of course. But, more importantly, you are creating space for your child and her journey through adolescence. And I can tell you that this process is going to take up quite a bit of that emotional headspace. You need to be intact for it, as centered and whole as you can be. Take care of yourself. Be gentle and non-judgmental with yourself. Raising a teenager today is not for the faint of heart, so you will need to be solid and strong as you embark on this journey with her. And she needs to know that you are there to lean on, to carry some of the emotional weight for her, through the toughest steps of the journey.

So, you need to key in on those areas in which you are overly self-critical, and just about every parent I know holds some degree of ongoing self-deprecation. The idea here is to grab hold of that elusive thought, that core belief, you hold about yourself. In your mind, are you a good enough parent? Do you feel capable, competent, and necessary yourself? Do you fear that you are, in some way, poisoning the well for your child?

If these questions reflect your beliefs about yourself, begin to work toward resolving them. Keep in mind that a parent's insecurities often mirror those of their children. So, if you can resolve some of this for yourself, you may be doing it for her as well. That is, she may question her own worth less if you do the same for yours.

Finally, here's something you can do right this moment: make a conscious choice to light up for your child the next time you see her. Let her see the light in your eyes that lets her know you love her unconditionally. After all, in most everything we've talked about, this is fundamentally what she is seeking: that unconditional positive regard, that feeling that she is okay, and important, and necessary, even if her life feels awful right now. This may be the most important thing we can do for our children in any given moment, period.

That's your job.

If you do this and only this, many other parenting sins will pass by forgiven or wholly unnoticed. Because the positive regard of lighting up trumps just about anything, especially in those dark moments when she feels worthless. Your light matters. And whatever gets in the way of shining that light needs to be cleared out any way you can, like an emotional weed whacker. This is great news for parents: You do not need to control the narrative. You just need to bear witness, and light up.

The indelible, critical underlying message here: "I see you."

That message is priceless.

I can imagine that much of this mandate feels overwhelming to you right now. But if you break it all down, and take it in steps, it will work. It does not, by the way, need to be perfect. You don't have to be perfect to be present. With each of these suggestions, your child will just get the idea, with increasing clarity, that you are available to them through their adolescence. And that is the goal here, plain and simple.

You can do this.

When Your Kid Seems Awful

The narrative is that the teenage years are horrible for parents. Our kids become sullen, mysterious, vulgar, moody, experimental, and uncooperative. The goal is to just get through it. I suspect that this read does very little to reverse that image. Your child is going to be awful and ruin your life. But now, this guy's telling me that adolescence is stretched even longer than expected. Your child will be awful forever.

No, that's not how it's going to go.

But as you've read, adolescence is an ever-so-stressful time today. Your child's attitude will, at times, manifest that stress. She may even seem flat-out awful at times.

Your job is to hang in with her, even in the awful moments. How mighty and noble and warrior-like it is as a parent to stay in the game, and hang in with your child, in the face of a slammed door, or rejection, or a wretched attitude. Because when they come to you, they let their guard down. They vent. They transfer, or download, a day's worth of stress and fear and identity traffic and anxiety into the safest place they know: you.

Taking it personally might seem at times a very natural reaction. But you've got to fight that reaction and hang in. Because even if she tells you she hates you, she does not hate you. Let her know she is not going to chase you out of her world. You are not going anywhere. Even if she's awful.

It is a mighty parent who can carry that weight for their child, who can recognize that she cannot carry it all alone, and who is available for the download, without taking it personally. The cycle of argument and dissonance and screaming might be a daily pattern in your home. You may wonder how you raised such an awful, unkind person.

The warrior parent recognizes this is not the process at play here. Instead, it is a very important emotional download, masquerading as an awful child.

If you can hang in with her, and you feel as if your connection is not improving and your kid isn't coming around, please wait her out. She will get there. She will just need to recondition her mind to reintegrate the concept of you as an ally. And that may take a moment. If you can navigate this process with humor, light and love, you clear some of the traffic within her overly busy mind. Take it from her, and release it. This way, you can liberate the both of you.

And even when your child is trying to draw you into an argument, you are allowed to opt out yourself, and I encourage you to do so, frequently. The emotional download is an adaptation of sorts. And it is certainly good news if your child is saving her "awfulness" for her time at home with you. This is far more adaptive than exhibiting such behavior at school, with teachers, coaches, or bosses, or perhaps even with her friends. Still, the download is not a behavior you want to encourage in your child, nor how she should cope well into adulthood. And you do not want your awful teenager to become an awful wife, or husband, or parent herself.

So, at a moment of calm, talk about the way you are going to help her negotiate any difficult moments. Let her know you are available for a calm and rational download, a discussion of whatever might be bothering her. Teaching her to talk through her feelings, instead of downloading them in an unhealthy manner, is paramount here. There is an element of modeling here, of course, as well. But this is also an opportunity to teach your child how to treat others in her life, even at times of stress. That's no small thing.

I have worked with a number of parents who have, quite courageously, admitted to me that they did not like their child very much at times. Upon reflection, we tend to find that what a parent dislikes about her child is a reflection of something she dislikes about herself. The dislike is, in essence, a projection, but a dangerous one. This is why it is so important that we as parents conduct our due diligence on our own emotional house, and clear away any clutter that may interfere with our connection with our kids.

Now, for most teenagers today, there is a hidden but very important skill woven into the ways in which they manage their relationships with you.

I work with an eighteen-year-old boy, James, who is a remarkably effective negotiator with his parents. When pressed to do more homework before going out with friends, for instance, he will point out that he has already done the homework due over the next couple of days or that he will have time to complete his work when he returns home. He asks, "Why?" way more frequently than his parents would like and typically has a ready retort. Like any good lawyer, he tends to know the answer before he asks the question and has his rebuttal well-prepared. He is smart, articulate, and thoughtful in these proceedings. Mom and Dad and I have talked at length about this presentation, and we agree that, though we want James to do his work on a more timely basis, his skill at discussion, debate, and negotiation will prove highly useful for him throughout life. We therefore do not want to discourage the discourse. We may want him to do as he's asked more frequently, to be sure. But we want to preserve what's special and unique about him in the process.

I find that this young man's set of skills is not at all uncommon and often makes up part of the narrative when we talk about our awful teenagers. Let's not forget those things that not only make them unique, but prepare them to take on the world. We want to recognize, acknowledge, and support those attributes.

Hope for the Future

You need to remember that kids today think differently than they ever have before. They have vision. They are future-oriented, and the picture they hold of their future is an integral component of their senses of self-worth. Too often, I find that parents are far too cavalier in the ways they present their own visions of their child's future to them. Jokes about carrying her financially for a lifetime, or that she will be a basement couch-dweller, run far too rampant in the family schtick.

You can stem the tide of an awful lot of your child's negative thinking about herself by attending to this issue specifically. If you give your child the message that she does not possess whatever she needs to be successful, she will, more likely than not, manifest your vision of no-confidence. Too often, I can see this in kids who bear themselves silently and slump-shouldered, lacking confidence and often, in their perception, even luck. If you compare your child negatively to one of their siblings, that is devastating. I promise you that even passing references to your child being "not good enough" are not at all benign and will be integrated into their thinking about themselves. The child you think is paying the least attention, or who never listens to a thing you say, is actually hearing your messages quite well and registering them clearly. All of your children are highly suggestible to your thoughts about them.

By the time many kids reach the threshold of my office, enough of these negative messages spawn a distinct, and fairly solid, sense of hopelessness. This hopelessness has often developed into actual symptoms of depression, anxiety, learned helplessness, attention issues, and so on. Subconsciously, parents promote this maladaptive, self-defeating pattern frequently.

It allows kids precious little to work with in developing a positive sense of self.

The message that she is not enough in any way—her intelligence, her athleticism, her body, her ability to connect socially—is something you can eliminate from your parenting repertoire right now, today. Pause, for just a moment, and think about the scope of your child's mindset, and whether you are poisoning it with negative messages about her or fueling it with positive messages of hope. Please keep in mind that both her current well-being and her vision for the future rely in very large part on your words and the vibe you present. So truly consider the words you choose, and choose them wisely. Create hope, and you are moving solidly in the right direction as a parent.

Attending to Your Messages

If you need a guideline here, let's borrow a concept I use when working with couples in conflict. In those situations, I encourage partners to consider their words so very carefully, such that they actually speak only 25 percent of the words that pass through their minds. I cannot stress enough how effective this is. It can be stilted and awkward at first, but that's a bargain when contrasted with hastily chosen, hurtful language piled up on itself. So, if you fear you may be denting your child's sense of self-worth with your words, take a moment and cut out 75 percent. I strongly suspect that the remaining 25 percent will buoy your child up with hope.

This is no small thing. This may not be everything, but man, it's close.

A Note to Dads

More than twenty years ago, I completed my dissertation on the gender roles of parents. Back then, it was clear that moms not only did the lion's share of housework but also were in charge of virtually all of the responsibilities of parenting. This comprises attending parent-teacher conferences, serving as the Uber driver, making lunches, and helping with homework. It also encapsulates the emotional care of each child, sitting and working through the fallout of disappointment, a failed test, a breakup, or other social issue. Moms stayed up to help with homework or studying. They were the go-to for parenting issues. Part of the argument then was that dads were the ones, for the most part, working full-time outside the home, so the division of labor made some sense.

This argument fell apart, I learned, when it became apparent that moms did the lion's share of parenting even when both parents were working or when Dad was the primary caregiver. Think about that. Two decades ago, even if Dad was home all day with the kids, Mom did most of the work of parenting.

I'm heartened to report that things have changed over the course of the last twenty years. Now, dads do far more at home, including housework and parenting. Dads are more involved in the lives of their kids than any generation preceding them, and this finding suggests enormous progress. I see more dads bringing their kids into therapy sessions now than ever before, supporting these findings. There are more dads in the audience when I speak at parenting events. Still, the formula is way out of balance, with moms remaining primary caregivers by a significant margin.

We dads need to get far more involved in the lives of our kids. We do not have the luxury of opting out or relinquishing the entirety of the parenting role to Mom. There are several reasons our voices, as dads and men, need to be in the mix for our kids. First, we are another adult who can be fully available, and our kids cannot have enough advocates as they navigate the storms of adolescence. These are also interesting times in terms of gender dynamics. Roles are shifting, and those men asserting alleged "power" over women are finally being held accountable. Your supportive voice here is critical, for both your girls and your boys. They need to hear your thoughts on the changing tide, and see you treat Mom, and other women in your life, with respect, dignity, and equality.

Your voice also falls differently than Mom's voice. Your children need to hear the contrast and learn those lessons you hold and may have learned through experience. They can learn so much from your stories, and your story will live on in them. Why would we ever relinquish any of that?

Along with the shift in gender dynamics, we are in the midst of change with regard to the definition and meaning of masculinity. We have referred to toxic masculinity and the sometimes invisible and unspoken negative effects it can wield, not just societally, but particularly the damage it can do to women. It's an important and exciting time to be a dad, as we get to be a part of the sweep of change. We can bring a gentleness, a loving, caring fatherhood, to this next generation. We can model the strength that comes with kindness and vulnerability for our boys and guide our girls to be vigilant for these qualities in their partners. For our LGBTQ children, we can add to the level of love and acceptance and comfort they receive from family. All of our kids are less at risk, in every way we've discussed, when we as dads are more involved.

This is the most important work we will ever do in our lives, guys. It's where the joy is, and what will keep us young. Don't give it away. You'll miss all the good stuff and wonder why you are burning out. Parenting can be tough at times; just ask a mom. But nothing we do will ever be more rewarding.

PARENTING AS A SPIRITUAL PRACTICE

I am in business in large part because, due to the radical shift in our culture, the spiritual practice of parenting is something that gets lost in the morass. I want you to take a moment and think back, back before your child was a teenager, to when she was young, little, innocent. Draw in a long, slow breath, and allow yourself to remember her. Man, you felt nothing but love for her then, right? If you sit with it, you can remember some times when the gorgeousness of her very being overwhelmed you. You could hardly believe you had anything to do with her being here, drawing breath, leaving you in awe of her bright and searching eyes, her thoughtful looks, her impossibly simple and open mind. The deep, spiritual connection with her likely required no effort on your part. It was easy, natural, organic, and undeniable. Such a sweet, sweet time to revisit.

That deep and spiritual connection remains available to you and your child to this day. Too often, however, I find it lies dormant, hidden beneath layers of anxious noise, waiting to be rediscovered.

Your kids are aware of that connection too, and that it feels different now. I cannot tell you how many teenagers have sat in my office describing the shift in their parents as they hit middle school and high school. The time spent connecting, talking, and laughing has diminished greatly and, in far too many families, entirely. Instead, parenting becomes pragmatic, a role we play. And rather suddenly, to our children, we become alien, disconnected and robotic. Too often, kids tell me they feel like résumé fodder for their parents, report cards on their ability to rear a proper adult. They feel as if they have become inconvenient, unacceptable stressors for their parents.

And when our kids become stressors, we effectively disconnect from them and, in a sense, dehumanize them. The result is that we whittle down our definition of success to match the narrowest, least interesting definition. We no longer sit proudly when our child exhibits behavior outside the mainstream. And we unwittingly break the most brilliant spirits.

But when you hold a deep and spiritual connection, there's this celebration of your child that you put forth, just like you did so easily when she was younger. If you can ease your parental anxiety, you hold that celebratory light together. It forms an indelible and lifelong bond that cannot be broken by the most vicious storms of life's experience. It's the secret essence of your connection, and she can lean on that connection hard when that grade falls, or she doesn't make the cut, or that bully posts, or that date blows her off, or she just does not like the way she looks. She knows you see her, that *perfect* her. And just knowing that light glows, that deep and spiritual connection, she can breathe. Together, you create the light that provides the strength to go on.

This connection is bigger than kindness and the most important, critical part of being a parent.

And trust me, the parent, now, of an adult. If you continue to hold that light, you will find that same comfort in it, regardless of geography or your own life's challenges. The benefit becomes twofold, as you are both carried by that light for a lifetime. That's spirit. It's esoteric, and tough to define, but you both know it when it's there.

See, this parenting thing, it shouldn't be hard. It can't be. It has got to be joyful. There are too many land mines awaiting your child that will be difficult. You want them to know that the light you carry together cannot, and will not, be dimmed by any such woes or disappointments. Curating this spiritual connection, keeping that light shining brightly on the most overcast of days, this is the mighty task, and joy, available to the parent of a teenager.

Let it shine.

ACKNOWLEDGEMENTS

Deepest gratitude to:

The patient and tireless Brenda Knight and the brilliant editing and marketing teams at Mango Publishing.

All my friends, colleagues, and advocates who have listened intently, offered suggestions generously, and made this a joyful path, including Michael Hainey, Andrew Santella, Chad and Tiffany Owen, Heidi Stevens, Wendy Snyder, Molly Fay, Mary Carroll and George Dougherty, Bela Ghandi and Andrew Annacone, Ilene and Mark Collins, Lori and Bob Donahoe, Barb and Paul Baldassarre, Mary Lukens, Dave Burdick, and everyone else who has helped me along this journey.

Bill and Giuliana Rancic, Kelli and Kevin Hurley, and Todd Adams and Cathy Cassini Adams for their kindness and ongoing support.

My family, for their love and support, including Walt, Georgiana, Mike, Nancy, Mary Ellen, Gary, Tom, Lynne, Garrett, Torie, Melissa, Jack, Grace, Claire, Rachel, Ken, Shirley, Jeff, Dave, Brad, Rochelle, and Chloe.

George Duffy for filling in blanks, and injecting love and humor, within these pages and in my life.

My co-author, co-editor, and partner-in-all-things, Julie Duffy. Thank you for your time, your intelligence, your expertise, and your love. You always add color and light to the darkness. I love you.

Finally, all the kids and families who have let me into their lives and shared their stories with me. Your work will help so many other families. These pages are blank without you.

ABOUT THE AUTHOR

Dr. Duffy is a highly sought-after clinical psychologist, bestselling author, podcaster, and parenting and relationship expert. He has been working in his clinical practice with individuals, couples, teens, and families for nearly twenty-five years. Dr. Duffy's refreshing and unique approach has provided the critical intervention and support needed to help thousands of individuals and families find their footing.

Along with his clinical work, Dr. Duffy is the author of the number-one bestselling *The Available Parent* (Viva Editions, second edition released 2014). He is a nationally recognized expert in parenting, teens, and relationships. He served as the regular parenting and relationship expert on *Steve Harvey*, with more than seventy-five appearances, and shares his expertise several times a month on WGN Radio. He also appears frequently on other national and local television and radio outlets and is cited regularly in national print and online publications. These include the *Today* show, Fox News, *Chicago Tribune*, *Fox Good Day Chicago*, *The Jam*, WGN-TV, *The Morning Blend*, NPR, the *Huffington Post*, the *Wall Street Journal*, *Redbook*, *Time*, *Good Housekeeping*, *Men's Health*, *Chicago Parent*, *Cosmopolitan*, *Teen Vogue*, *Wired*, *Parenting*, *Your Teen*, *Parents*, *Family Circle*, *Chicago Sun-Times*, and *Real Simple* magazine, among many others.

Dr. Duffy is cohost of a popular podcast, better, with his wife Julie, as well as *On Purpose* with *Chicago Tribune* columnist Heidi Stevens.

Mango Publishing, established in 2014, publishes an eclectic list of books by diverse authors—both new and established voices—on topics ranging from business, personal growth, women's empowerment, LGBTQ studies, health, and spirituality to history, popular culture, time management, decluttering, lifestyle, mental wellness, aging, and sustainable living. We were recently named 2019's #1 fastest growing independent publisher by Publishers Weekly. Our success is driven by our main goal, which is to publish high quality books that will entertain readers as well as make a positive difference in their lives.

Our readers are our most important resource; we value your input, suggestions, and ideas. We'd love to hear from you—after all, we are publishing books for you!

Please stay in touch with us and follow us at:
Facebook: Mango Publishing
Twitter: @MangoPublishing
Instagram: @MangoPublishing
LinkedIn: Mango Publishing
Pinterest: Mango Publishing

Sign up for our newsletter at www.mango.bz and receive a free book! Join us on Mango's journey to reinvent publishing, one book at a time.